THE BUSINESS GUIDE TO
Credit
Management

Cash in on our experience.

Making change happen is one thing; making it stick is quite another. Many businesses have made cash their focus, but maintaining results depends on management leading and embedding behaviours across the entire business.

Talk to us about how to maintain cash behaviours, and how we can help you stay ahead.

Visit us now at pwc.co.uk/rmg

THE BUSINESS GUIDE TO
Credit Management

Advice and solutions for cash-flow control, financial risk and debt management

Consultant Editor:
Jonathan Reuvid

RECOMMENDED BY
INSTITUTE OF DIRECTORS

KoganPage

LONDON PHILADELPHIA NEW DELHI

This book has been endorsed by the Institute of Directors.

The endorsement is given to selected Kogan Page books which the IoD recognizes as being of specific interest to its members and providing them with up-to-date, informative and practical resources for creating business success. Kogan Page books endorsed by the IoD represent the most authoritative guidance available on a wide range of subjects including management, finance, marketing, training and HR.

The views expressed in this book are those of the authors and are not necessarily the same as those of the Institute of Directors.

Publisher's note

Every possible effort has been made to ensure that the information contained in this book is accurate at the time of going to press, and the publishers and authors cannot accept responsibility for any errors or omissions, however caused. No responsibility for loss or damage occasioned to any person acting, or refraining from action, as a result of the material in this publication can be accepted by the editor, the publisher or any of the authors.

First published in Great Britain and the United States in 2010 by Kogan Page Limited

120 Pentonville Road
London N1 9JN
United Kingdom
www.koganpage.com

525 South 4th Street, #241
Philadelphia PA 19147
USA

4737/23 Ansari Road
Daryaganj
New Delhi 110002
India

© Kogan Page, Jonathan Reuvid and individual contributors, 2010

The right of Kogan Page, Jonathan Reuvid and individual contributors to be identified as the authors of this work has been asserted by them in accordance with the Copyright, Designs and Patents Act 1988.

ISBN   978 0 7494 5978 9
E-ISBN   978 0 7494 5979 6

British Library Cataloguing-in-Publication Data

A CIP record for this book is available from the British Library.

Library of Congress Cataloging-in-Publication Data

Reuvid, Jonathan.
   The business guide to credit management : advice and solutions for cost control, financial risk management and capital protection / Jonathan Reuvid. – 1st ed.
      p. cm.
   ISBN 978-0-7494-5978-9 – ISBN 978-0-7494-5979-6 1. Credit–Management. 2. Cost control. 3. Risk management. I. Title.
   HG3751.R48 2010
   658.8'8–dc22
                              2010005213

Typeset by Saxon Graphics Ltd, Derby
Printed and bound in Great Britain by MPG Books Ltd, Bodmin, Cornwall

With Invoice Finance you don't have to wait to be paid.

Late payment is the last thing a small business needs. With Invoice Finance, we can pay up to 90% of the value of your invoices within 24 hours of you raising them (fee applies). We can also collect money on your behalf, freeing you up to get on with your business. Also, with our optional Bad Debt Protection, if a customer becomes insolvent you could receive up to 100% of what you're owed, so you can take on new clients with confidence. Invoice Finance – just one of the ways we're **here for you.**

To find out more, contact your Relationship Manager, visit www.rbsif.co.uk or call 0800 711 911. Minicom 0800 404 6160. Calls may be recorded.

Contents

of any disputes. In many cases this improves customer retention. Most external agencies are traditionally used as a last resort, but Vilcol has found that being used this early increases the overall collections success rate by a factor of between 8-10 times, compared to tertiary work from the same client.

OUR PEOPLE

The 51 staff based in Surrey is the backbone of the business. They make it work. Vilcol pays a lot of attention to its people. When other similar business were getting into price wars and firing staff to reduce costs, Vilcol chose instead to focus on its people and develop the best customer care package in the industry.

This meant that they had to invest a lot in terms of time, money and technology. This does not mean that as an organisation they are foolproof, but the business objectives for 2010 is to get things right the first time. With a series of incentives and a no ceiling on income policy, the people at Vilcol are highly motivated to do their very best.

As an example, the trace manager completed a Dale Carnegie Management Course; the collection manager became a member of the Credit management institute. Six agents in the debt recovery team at the same time asked to take the NVQ in Debt Recovery Course. There is a continuous improvement culture in Vilcol it is a believer in lifelong learning.

OUR AIMS

Steve Rowlands the Managing Director of Vilcol says, "We aim to provide the best service possible to all - our staff, our partners and their customers. For example, we recognise that not every debtor has a bank account, so we invested in the Vilcol Easy payment Card System, a simple payment system that allows a certain type of debtor to pay their bills at the local corner shop, post office, etc. Our commercial debtors are also offered a full payment facilities, including company credit card acceptance (at no charge to the client) and instant payments by BAC'S. In fact Vilcol has signed up to the Better payment Practice Code which is another way to collect debts, interest and collection costs."

"We make it as easy as possible for people to pay. By doing so, we help the debtor; we help the customers because they get more of their money back and we help ourselves, because we continue to gain revenue; a win, win situation."

"By paying attention to everyone's needs, I believe we will continue to outperform all our competitors, all of whom are considerably bigger than us, and gain a ranking in the top five. Not bad for an agency that, only three years ago, was ranking around 247. I believe we can and so does everyone who works here. The team spirit is, in my opinion, probably the best in the industry."

OUR SUCCESS

Steve Rowlands will continue to serve on a government advisory committee for Small Businesses. Vilcol also represents the credit industry on the CBI committee consulting with the Home Office on the introduction of new national Identity Card. In 2007 Vilcol was nominated for a Business Achievement Award for 'Services for Debt Recover 2007' by Today Magazine. Steve said that, "I am more pleased that we have been re-accredited for both ISO 9001-2002 and Investing In People, than winning a new business award. This shows that our people continue to produce quality work and give customer satisfaction, you can win only so many awards"

Vilcol won the British Small Business Champion Award 2002 for southern England. Prior to attending the awards ceremony, Steve met the Prime Minister and Small Business Minister, Nigel Griffiths, at 10 Downing Street for a reception to mark the achievement of all the finalists.

Nigel Griffiths said: "Steve typifies the British small business managing director – someone that does not often get the headlines but is one of the unsung heroes of the economy. That is why I'm delighted to support these awards. Being a finalist gives business like Steve's the recognition it deserves. Both the Prime Minister and myself congratulate Steve on his nomination."

Vilcol were finalists in the 2008 debt Collection Agency of the year sponsored by the Credit Today Magazine.

Since the start of the millennium Vilcol has won 6 business awards.

WHAT IS NEW IN 2010?

Vilcol is continuing to establish its specialist agency status, in the UK debt collection market as many of its competitors unfortunately go out of business.

Why is Vilcol better at recoveries than the competition? We use our well-known skill at manually tracing persistent debtors in combination with the plethora of new public domain Internet search engines to give the best tracing results. While continuing to develop the ability of our people, to negotiate with debtors to get part payments as more and more people want a slice of their out goings. Our recovery team also agrees significantly higher settlements and more payments in full, than most of our rivals.

Our new method of negotiating settlements has significantly improved our collection success rates. Especially when combined with our revolutionary new way of paying clients quickly, called Advance Collection Payments which is Vilcol's alternative to debt purchase.

Vilcol and Vilcollections are the trading styles of Village Investigations Limited, which is a wholly owned private company. It is not part of a group of companies.

Phone: +44 (0)1925 816-626
Fax: +44 (0)1925 853-432
E-Mail: info@eos-solutions.uk.com
Web: www.eos-solutions.uk.com

Successful together

'With head and heart' – this is the principle that EOS experts follow, working in partnership with companies of all sizes in all industries to ensure their survival – and not just in economically difficult times.

Anyone coming out of the lift on the twelfth floor of EOS headquarters will catch their breath at the fabulous view of Hamburg – the port city and Germany's gateway to the world. And anyone wanting to acquire customers, conclude a contract with partners they haven't worked with before, market products securely over the Internet or deal with defaulting payers will have come to the right address. Over 4000 EOS employees help companies throughout the world to set up profitable, long-term business relationships by providing professional receivables management, turning outstanding sums of money into revenue. They also offer risk information and marketing information as well as electronic payment system solutions.

The roots of this international group – that consists today of more than 40 companies in over 20 countries – go back to Deutscher Inkasso-Dienst (DID) founded in 1974 by OTTO, the German multi-channel retailer. Nowadays, these specialist companies operate together under the umbrella of EOS, a wholly owned subsidiary of the Otto Group. They combine regional expertise with international know-how, providing a broad range of products from a single point of contact. In the UK, the local EOS company offers arrears management, asset retrieval, credit management, overdue account management, debt recovery, debt collection, litigation and outstanding account conclusion.

Preventing money shortages

Stuart Knock, Managing Director of EOS Solutions UK, knows why targeted receivables management is such a decisive factor. 'Many companies worry about alienating their customers or they lack internal capacities, which is why they do not follow up outstanding payments consistently enough, or send any reminders.' Yet every overdue payment costs money. Four per cent of British companies have even encountered cash flow problems as a result of delayed payments or non-payment. This is one result of the EOS Five Nations Survey 2009 'European Payment Practices' in which EOS questioned 200 companies in the United Kingdom on their payment experiences.

With EOS, companies can make advance provisions. 'We train our employees intelligently and professionally so that they can deal with defaulting payers,' Mr Knock points out. They regularly check the deadlines, draft individual reminders and talk to people over the phone and in person. 'We are only satisfied if we can find solutions that are just as accommodating for our clients as for their customers,' says the Managing Director.

Contact
EOS Solutions UK • 2 Birchwood Office Park • Crab Lane, Fearnhead • Warrington WA2 0XS

List of Contributors

Niall Cooter is a Senior Manager at PricewaterhouseCoopers (PwC) specializing in releasing cash from working capital. He has advised more than 150 clients throughout Europe and the USA from a broad range of industries. Prior to joining PwC in 1999, Niall spent 13 years with a working capital consulting firm.

PwC working capital specialists provide advisory and outsourcing solutions to help clients to release their cash and excess cost from working capital operations. They draw on industry knowledge and cultural expertise of more than 150,000 people in 153 countries across the PwC network to provide seamless global solutions for their clients.

Xavier Denecker has been the Managing Director of Coface in the UK & Ireland since October 2007. Xavier has a wide background in banking and international business and credit insurance. He joined Coface Group in 1990 as Communications Director, and then developed Coface business in Italy as well as Spain and Portugal, having been Managing Director of the Iberian platform for seven years.

Coface has been a leading provider of credit management in the United Kingdom and Republic of Ireland since 1993, providing a local service from offices in London, Dublin, Watford, Birmingham, Leeds and Cardiff. The company's offering integrates credit assessment, collection services and cover for unpaid debts while multinational businesses can protect their worldwide subsidiaries through Coface's international network. Coface provides working capital and off balance sheet facilities to complement its product line, as well as access to domestic and international business information and a collection network at home and overseas. Coface is also a recognized operator in the London political risk market and a provider of surety bonds and guarantees.

Peter Finlayson heads up the Policy Division at the Payments Council, the organization established in 2007 to set strategy for UK payments and ensure UK payment systems and services meet the needs of users, payment service providers and the wider economy. In this capacity he is involved in a wide range of strategic and policy issues concerning future developments in the UK payments industry. He and his team were instrumental in the formulation of the National Payments Plan and are responsible for its delivery.

Simon Hampton is a Director of TAK-Outsourcing Limited. TAK provides outsourced credit control services, helping businesses to become more profitable by collecting their cash faster. He has over 25 years' experience covering HR, payroll and finance, working most recently for Xchanging plc, a fast-growing international business process outsourcing company based in the City of London. TAK Credit Management is a trading name of TAK-Outsourcing Limited.

John Holmes is an English Solicitor practising international law at the Amsterdam office of Dutch law firm Bierens Incasso Advocaten BV; other offices are located in Veghel, the Netherlands, Barcelona, Dusseldorf and Paris.

Philip King was appointed Chief Executive of the Institute of Credit Management (ICM) in January 2006, having previously played a number of local and national roles within the organization since graduating in 1980. In addition to his ICM qualification, he holds the Certified Diploma in Accounting and Finance and an MBA from Strathclyde Graduate Business School. Prior to taking up his post at the ICM, Philip had 26 years' practical experience in credit management with STC Distributors, Olivetti and finally with Vodafone, where he worked for 10 years. Philip King sits on a number of industry- and government-led bodies and speaks extensively on the importance of cash flow and credit management, on which he is regularly quoted. He was the author of a series of *Managing Cashflow Guides* written by the ICM for BIS (formerly BERR) in 2008.

Zoe Lacey is Head of Collections & Recoveries at Mint Credit Management UK Ltd and has been with the company since 2006. An Associate Member of the Institute of Credit Management (AICM), she is responsible for leading the commercial and consumer debt recovery teams and liaising with clients to ensure that they receive the highest possible levels of service. Zoe has a specialized expertise in managing high-volume contracts and consistently achieves high levels of recovery success. After graduating with a BA(Hons) in 1999, Zoe pursued a career in management accounting and continued her personal development, becoming a Chartered Institute of Management Accountants (CIMA) student.

Stewart Lund is a Chartered Accountant and a director of Resolvent Ltd with 20 years of experience in helping small and medium-sized businesses to grow. Stewart has performed numerous executive and non-executive roles in many industries including telecommunications, construction and media.

Resolvent Ltd specialize in providing support and advice to small and medium-sized businesses to help them throughout the business life cycle, including long-term non-executive roles, corporate rescue and turnaround work, soft debt collection, advice on insolvency and directors' liabilities and contract negotiation.

Ross McFarlane started his career in invoice finance in 1986 with Alex Lawrie Factors. He joined RBS in 1988, working for The Royal Bank of Scotland Invoice Finance (RBSIF) initially as a Business Development Manager based in Glasgow, where he was also instrumental in establishing the Scottish Operations Centre. In 1994 Ross was appointed UK Sales Manager and moved to the then Head Office in Croydon. During the next four years Ross reinvigorated the marketing strategy, which helped RBSIF to double its market share, and was appointed Sales Director in 1998.

Following the integration of RBSIF and the Nat West business of Lombard Commercial Services, Ross was appointed Regional Director for London, before taking up the role of Director UK Sales & Client Relations. With a career of over 20 years within invoice finance, he has wide experience of developing working capital solutions for business and in helping them through a full range of economic cycles.

Shaun Maloney is Sales Director at TALKINGtech UK, and is responsible for account management and strategy across the United Kingdom, Europe and South Africa. His work has been focused predominantly on the credit and collections industry in the Finance division, consulting at senior management level with the leading UK banking, telecom and utilities brands on automated contact strategies, proactive customer care programmes and call reduction initiatives. Shaun's career includes five years as Vice President – Product and Marketing with Citibank Consumer Bank and, more recently, during a year's sabbatical from TALKINGtech to consult for AXA New Zealand in the restructuring of their national distribution and customer service channels and process.

For over 20 years, TALKINGtech has been a specialist in Interactive Voice Messaging (IVM) and Interactive Voice Response (IVR) design, development and hosting. It has built a reputation in the wider credit and collections industry as a valuable contributor in contact centre resource studies and customer contact strategies.

Brett Marlow is the owner of Jobs in Credit and created the concept of the company Web Recruitment Services Limited, which runs two leading jobs boards; www.jobsincredit.com and www.jobsinrisk.com, after more than 10 years' experience working within the credit industry for Dun & Bradstreet and Experian in senior sales positions. Launched in 2004, both sites offer excellent-quality candidates working within all areas of credit, collections, risk and compliance at a fraction of the cost of traditional recruitment methods.

Charles Mayhew is a Director and shareholder of Moreton Smith, based in Central London. A Member of the Institute of Credit Management (MICM), he has spent the last 16 years in the credit management industry, working during that time with two large privately owned collection agencies.

Moreton Smith provides bespoke solutions to collect overdue debt both on a domestic and international basis. The company also provides credit control outsourcing in 22 languages and award-winning credit management hosted software.

George Miles is Managing Director of Paladin Commercial Credit Management. A credit management professional for 25 years, he held several senior positions at Unicol – Interim Justicia before becoming the founding director Paladin Commercial in 1995. He has been the driving force behind Paladin's success over the past 14 years and has forged strong partnerships with an impressive list of clients.

George is also an industry champion for best practice and is often involved in workshops and forums for the Association of Credit Professionals (ACP), where he is a board member. He is also an authorized lecturer for the government-backed initiative 'debtored', which helps educate young students in money management, credit and banking.

Joyce Newman has over 20 years' experience in debt collection and purchase. She is one of the founding directors of Lowell Group, formed in 2004 and now widely acknowledged as the United Kingdom's leading debt purchasing company. As Group Sales & Marketing Director, Joyce is responsible for establishing and maintaining relationships with existing debt sellers and identifying new debt sale opportunities. She is also integrally involved in the execution of purchases.

In both 2008 and 2009 Lowell Group was ranked No 1 in the OC&C index of all the main credit management and debt collection companies in the United Kingdom, taking account of both past performance and future strategy. In 2009, employing 400 people at its state-of-art HQ and customer contact centre in Leeds, the Group was also placed second in the Sunday Times Deloitte league table of Britain's 100 private equity-backed companies with the fastest growing profits.

Trevor Philips is Director of PreLegal Services and Director of Sales and Marketing at Lovetts plc. He trained originally as a credit manager and has 40 years' experience in credit management, having served in various roles at AMF International, the Galliford Group, UAPT Infolink, Equifax and Commercial Collection Services. In 1998 Trevor established Credit Professionals Limited and accepted a number of non-executive positions in industry. Key amongst these was a consultancy at Lovetts plc, a leading commercial debt recovery firm of solicitors where he now has responsibility for Sales and Marketing and heads up the International Prelegal Services division. He was presented with the Special Award for Outstanding Services to the Credit Industry in 1996. He retired from the ICM Council in 2003 after 26 years, having served as Treasurer, Vice Chairman and National Chairman between 1987 and 1993 and then as Vice President from 1995 until his retirement. He is well known on the lecture circuits and has chaired many of the credit conferences held over the last few years.

Vernon Phillips is Chief Executive of the High Court Enforcement Officers Association. He was previously Executive Director of the Enforcement Services Association. Vernon has also been a civil servant, working for both the Department for Education and the Lord Chancellor's Department (now the Ministry of Justice).

The High Court Enforcement Officers Association is the professional representative body for Authorised High Court Enforcement Officers. It represents its members and regularly consults with central government on legislative proposals, as well as working to maintain and develop standards of excellence throughout the profession.

Mike Purvis is Managing Director of Transcom Worldwide (UK), a leading provider of outsourced credit management, debt collection and customer management services.

Jonathan Reuvid is co-author of the *Handbook of International Trade* and the *Handbook of World Trade*, the editor of *Managing Business Risk* and is the editor and part-author of investment guides to China, the 10 countries that joined the EU in 2004 and Morocco. Before taking up a second career in business publishing he was Sales and Marketing Director, then European Operations Director of the manufacturing subsidiaries of a Fortune 500 multinational. From 1984 until 2005 he engaged in joint venture development and start-ups in China through his consultancy, Hethe Management Services.

Graham Sands left the armed services in 1992 and worked in the credit industry for 10 years. He completed a Business Honours Degree in 2002, which facilitated his appointment as Group Credit Manager for a large international IT company. He now manages and directs his own successful credit management company, Amril Limited.

Amril is passionate about supporting businesses in building strong working relationships with their clients in order to reduce their late payments and increase their cash flow.

Amy Slayford is Client Experience Director at specialist trade credit broker Aon Trade Credit UK and has worked within the trade credit insurance industry for over 10 years. Amy works with the UK broking and development teams to help them deliver consistent value and service to their clients.

Aon's specialist trade credit team works with clients to design specific trade receivable solutions to meet their strategic business needs. Its dedicated team offers advice to support businesses to protect and finance their sales. Aon specializes in a range of products including credit insurance, trade finance, business information and credit diagnostic tools.

Maarten de Wild has been working in the credit management industry for more than 15 years and is responsible for the international sales activities within OnGuard. Globally, a lot of experience is gained in the credit management processes and procedures, the improvements and benefits across business lines and from SMEs to large corporates.

Martin Williams is Managing Director of Graydon UK and has spent the past 30 years in the credit information industry. Since 1991, he has also been a member of the Institute of Credit Management (ICM) and is a regular presenter and speaker at credit management forums in the United Kingdom. In 2008, at the invitation of Philip King, Director General of the ICM, Martin joined the ICM think tank (an expert panel of 20–25 industry leaders who meet quarterly and act as an influencing force on all issues related to the credit industry in the UK). In the same year and again in 2009, Martin Williams was honoured by *Credit Today* after being included in their Credit 100 list of people who have had the greatest impact in the credit industry during the year.

Owned by Atradius, Coface and Euler Hermes, three of Europe's leading credit insurance organizations, Graydon UK is one of the leading database information providers specializing in credit risk management. Graydon provides a complete, differentiated and high-quality package of credit risk management services with access to credit information and reports on companies in more than 190 countries worldwide.

Foreword

Miles Templeman, Director General of the Institute of Directors

If anyone was in doubt as to the paramount importance of cash flow to any business enterprise, whether great or small, the experience of the past three years – combining the cumulative effects of both the 'credit crunch' and a global recession – has hammered home a single vital lesson: make sure the practice of prudent financial management never lapses. From the more high-profile cases involving billions of pounds of toxic debt, through to SMEs who've seen sharp rises in the numbers of insolvent trading partners, the financial environment is now such that credit management has to be addressed and reviewed on a continual basis, and cannot be left to those who may lack the proper experience and training to co-ordinate and implement it effectively.

In challenging market conditions, directors and senior managers know that pruning operating costs severely and deferring capital expenditure are necessary corrective actions which will improve cash flow, albeit not always as quickly as may be hoped. However, more immediate relief can be gained by focusing on the current account parts of the balance sheet. Delaying payments to creditors is certainly one option, but there are standards of best practice which directors and managers will wish to observe; straying beyond supplier and service provider terms of business without prior agreement is likely to damage long-term business relationships. In order to avoid these perils, paying closer attention to the management of a company's own debtors must be a priority.

The Business Guide to Credit Management addresses both the simpler and more complex issues of managing the credit extended to customers and recovering any delayed payments without destroying either customer relationships or, where necessary, debt recovery. The central theme in all the advice given to readers by the credit management professionals who have authored this book – including contributions from key players such as PricewaterhouseCoopers, Coface and Graydon UK – is that effective credit management policies and processes must be at the very heart of any business operation. At the same time, enterprises need to install such procedures while times are good and not simply introduce them as a reaction to adverse business conditions.

As in most human affairs, prevention is better than cure and The Institute of Directors endorses this good advice wholeheartedly.

Preface

Philip King, Chief Executive of the Institute of Credit Management

Good credit management, and by definition good credit managers, have always been important, but in recent times such importance has taken on new meaning. 'Good' is almost not enough any more; 'Excellence' is what every credit manager should be striving for, and what the Institute of Credit Management helps its Members to attain.

Businesses always have to confront pressure on cash flow and limited access to finance. The role of the professional credit manager in keeping the cash flowing is becoming ever more critical.

Credit management can be defined simply as the policies and practices businesses follow in collecting payments from their customers. The credit manager is the individual tasked with setting these processes and ensuring they are effectively implemented. Modern credit managers proactively and positively input to many departments, functions and procedures to improve business flow and customer service, as well as focusing on their main role of protecting their organization's investment in debtors and recovering debt.

Their remit of course varies from organization to organization, and industry to industry, but is increasingly becoming much more strategic, given that large organizations are known to have strategies for either non-payment to help their own bottom-line profit, or at least significantly delaying payment, causing the supplier to finance them at no cost.

At its most fundamental, a credit manager will oversee the sales ledger function, including raising invoices in a timely and accurate manner, speedy cash posting and accurate allocation of that cash, agreeing invoice formats with larger customers, and ensuring sales teams are capturing data accurately to prevent subsequent invoice queries. In times of crisis, it is these 'fundamentals' that become more important than ever.

Credit managers may be assessing risk on new accounts and existing customers by way of credit information providers, reading financial accounts and establishing trading histories; they may be involved in creating a full credit policy – internal documents that identify all set and agreed procedures and policies that govern the credit function. They may also be agreeing terms of business with new and existing customers, including payment terms and setting up service level agreements and credit lines, and reporting to Directors on age and profile of debt, potential risks of bad debt, overtrading accounts, areas of suggested training and general customer service observations. They are also likely to be overseeing or monitoring the activities of tracing agents, debt collection agencies, solicitors, insolvency practitioners and other third parties.

As well as their direct 'financial' responsibilities, they are typically tasked with identifying system or software improvements and playing a key role in their implementation, documentation and the training of those who will be affected. They are also often responsible for motivating, coaching and setting targets for the credit team, usually collection targets, debtor day reduction targets, unallocated cash reduction targets and ongoing desk-side coaching to get the best out of each call and account contact.

Support is available to businesses, and to credit managers specifically, in various ways, and publications such as this *Business Guide to Credit Management* – covering a diverse range of subjects from best practice to new technology – make a valuable contribution to furthering their knowledge and understanding of what is an increasingly challenging and complex role.

Introduction

The current difficult business conditions suffered throughout the European Union, the United States and further afield are likely to persist throughout 2010 and beyond. In such times, the senior management of all enterprises, both big and small, are focusing their attention on credit management and how to improve their business performance. Published in association with the Institute of Directors (IoD) and the Institute of Credit Management (ICM), this new business guide addresses the issues involved.

The book is divided into five parts and all but the last chapter are written by credit industry professionals. Part One considers aspects of good practice in managing credit and includes contributions from PricewaterhouseCoopers and Amril, as well as Philip King, Chief Executive of ICM.

The topics of Part Two all relate to cash-flow improvement, the motivation for better credit management in business. Senior managers from Graydon UK, Transcom Worldwide and Lowell Group bring the experience of their organizations to bear on offering their best advice to readers on achieving this main objective.

In Part Three, the book focuses in more detail on methods and some innovative tools for managing credit successfully, with chapters from OnGuard Credit Management Software, Coface UK & Ireland, TALKINGtech and TAK-Outsourcing. Also included are chapters on job-hunting in the credit and collections industry by Jobs in Credit and on the professional enforcement of judgments from the High Court Enforcement Officers Association.

Part Four is devoted to the highly sensitive areas of customer relations and how to strike the difficult balance between limiting credit risk, effective debt collection and customer retention.

Part Five turns to the highly complex topics of cross-border debt recovery from export customers and the use of technology with contributions from Bierens Incasso Advocates and Moreton Smith, both leading practitioners in this field. We have added to this professional advice my own recommendations on how to limit risk in exports both in developed and developing markets. Appendix I provides supporting data for risk assessment in 10 selected export markets, provided by the online COFACE service as at 12 December 2009.

As publishers, Kogan Page offers its sincere thanks to the key sponsors, whose logos appear on the front cover and to the other contributing advertisers who have supported the book. I add my personal appreciation to all the authors who have written with clarity and insight to provide informative editorial.

Hopefully, we shall move forward into a recovery phase soon from the present low ebb in our business affairs, but there is little doubt that readers will want to continue with the improved credit management strategies and practices that they have developed during the period of economic reverse. In the ubiquitous words of government agencies and others that fail to deliver, 'lessons have been learnt'.

Jonathan Reuvid
December 2009

Part 1

Back to basics

Keeping control of your cash flow

Ross McFarlane, RBS Invoice Finance

The current economic pressures create new difficulties for small businesses as they struggle to manage cash flow in an uncertain market. Cash is the lifeblood of any business, and when the economy slows, and customers take longer to pay, it can be difficult to assess which of your customers will pay, or can pay. Payment terms can extend quite significantly and the likelihood of customers becoming insolvent and never paying increases. This uncertainty of cash flow can trip up even the most cautious and well-funded small business.

The government has helped small businesses with a range of initiatives, including the Enterprise Finance Guarantee Scheme (EFG), to bolster security to banks and to help them to support small business. Many banks have also taken steps to give comfort by providing fair and consistent pricing and confirming facilities for 12-month periods. As one of the banks in the middle of this debate, we are keen to ensure the facts are well understood and that small businesses recognize we are open for business and keen to help. We have a wealth of experience dealing with a wide range of businesses and have specialist skills to manage the working capital cycle with help to achieve faster payments with greater certainty.

Many businesses fail not from lack of profit, but from a lack of cash, because when the funds dry up, there is often nowhere else to go. That is why safe and certain receipt of funds from customers is the top priority. Business overdrafts can provide a pot of money to bridge the gap between paying for supplies and wages and receipt of money for trade sales, but something more closely involved and shaped to the working capital will provide fuller and safer support. All businesses should have disciplines to approve who they sell to, to fund the trade terms (typically 30–60 days), have effective credit control and have some form of protection in the event of bad debts. RBS Invoice Finance's (RBSIF's) approach is to provide businesses with a full end-to-end service to cover these aspects, which blends the options of invoice finance, factoring, or a complete package of asset-based lending. Small businesses often want to select from the range of services; perhaps they already have trade insurance, or perhaps a very strong credit controller, but often they appreciate support right throughout the working capital cycle. In particular, businesses need help in approving new customers, avoiding late payments and mitigating the risks of bad debts.

We encourage businesses to take a step-by-step approach and are happy to help with expertise at each stage.

1. Approve new customers

Businesses are always looking for new customers and new markets and should also be constantly reviewing the strength of existing customers. The dynamics change constantly, creating new risk and new opportunities, both at home and in export markets. Businesses should have a robust process to approve their customers, set appropriate credit limits and check this regularly. RBSIF uses up to six databases to confirm credit worthiness of a business's customers and has vast experience of dealing with late payments. This professional help can be invaluable when opening new markets and sustaining existing sales and helps to set a predictable pattern of sales receipts.

2. Fund invoiced sale

There is a wide range of finance on offer, and businesses can be attracted to the simplicity of an overdraft but this has limitations and does not link to the day-to-day receipts or delays in payments, and can be an uncertain line of finance in a challenging economy. One of the fullest types of support is invoice finance and since the invoice finance business provider is closely involved with all aspects of the working capital cycle, we have confidence to advance up to 85 per cent of sale proceeds as soon as these are invoiced. This will typically settle all costs of sales as soon as invoices are raised, leaving a business with funds to settle bills and get on with the next sale. The 15 per cent, which can typically be the gross profit, less charges, is available as soon as the invoice is paid. These facilities are available to advance the proceeds of domestic or export sales, also mitigating the risk of currency movements.

3. Collect invoices and credit control

A common problem affecting businesses is cash flow being squeezed when suppliers want payment for purchases quickly and yet customers demand longer payment terms or pay late. Skilled credit controllers will help and RBSIF have a team of over 60 credit controllers who exhaustively, but sensitively, pursue payment. Specialist collection teams will know who is paying and who is overdue and also have multilingual skills and legal assistance if necessary to achieve faster payments. Businesses should not underestimate the benefit of these skills. Even bringing payments forward by one week can generate £40,000 of working capital for a business with £2m annual turnover.

4. Protect from insolvency and avoid bad debts

A full end-to-end working capital service includes protection from bad debts. Businesses should be protected from the impact of bad debts, either by creating a wide spread of sales so that any single bad debt is not too damaging, or by taking some form of protection. This can be achieved with independent trade insurance, but RBSIF prefer to offer a 'joined-up' service to approve customers at the outset, keep in touch to monitor any slow payment and at the end of the line to provide protection from bad debts in the event of any insolvency. The benefits of a joined up approach from one supplier is that the end-to-end service is offered 24/7 on one simple web-based system supported by one local relationship manager.

5. Management information and constant attention

Businesses need to have robust systems and be able to answer 'yes' to having disciplines in place to approve, fund, collect and protect their invoiced sales. This is a tall order for small businesses relying only on overdraft finance and it can be far better to take a package of support that covers all of the working capital management, typically known as factoring with bad debt protection.

Working Capital Management facilities from RBS Invoice Finance offer a full service including:

■ credit approval of new and existing customers;
■ funding up to 85 per cent of sales invoices as soon as you issue the sales invoice, potentially more including government EFG support;
■ credit control, bringing payment forward 5–15 days in some circumstances;
■ protection from bad debts;
■ free cheque clearance and currency exchange;
■ signed agreement in simple language and with competitive pricing;
■ local Relationship Manager and award-winning web-based 24/7 communication.

Top tips to consider on common themes affecting small businesses

- Cash is king – keep control of your cash flow by having the right management information and systems in place. They'll allow you to act on warning signs before they become a problem. Take professional help.

- Talk to us – there is a lot of support available to small businesses. RBS have 2,300 local business managers offering customers free face-to-face advice. We also have a Business Hotline staffed by experienced bankers ready to talk, help, and offer free advice on how to secure support from your bank.

- Confirm the strength of your customers on a regular basis – take out credit references, or make enquiries of the payment records. Even a business that has traded with you for years may become more fragile in the current economic climate and may already be delaying payments to other businesses.

- Keep on top of payments and credit control -- businesses have been paying later in recent times. Chase payments on a structured basis and at least weekly. If payment is overdue do not hesitate to use legal advice and be sure to stop future supplies.

- Look at your costs – look at purchase costs as well as staffing and fixed costs. If sales fall, avoid taking on unprofitable business but do consider new areas. Cost each product or service to give you a picture of which products as well as which customers make a profit. The flip side of price is cost, and you can maintain profit margins even if you are reducing prices, provided you also reduce the costs of what you are making or providing.

- Look at new areas of business – each environment is different, but explore new opportunities, new markets and possibly exports. Work out the capital required and consider the payback, both short and medium term, or the impact of doing nothing.

- Protection – be sure to explore trade insurance or bad debt protection through factoring facilities.

- Spread your risk – small businesses can be built on the success of one key customer or just a small customer base. All it takes is for one customer to move to another supplier or even cease to trade and your business has immediate cash-flow problems because of the concentration.

Case Study 1 – New business breaks turnover targets supported by RBS

Fledgling Prestwich-based IT business is on course to record an £8m turnover in its first full year of trading – more than double its original turnover target.

IT Hardware & Software Ltd (ITHS) specializes in the sourcing and sale of IT hardware such as servers, hard drives, keyboards and monitors. To support the company's rapid growth RBSIF in Manchester provided the company with a £700,000 funding package.

ITHS was formed by David Warner and Alan Glazer, both of whom have substantial experience in buying and selling IT systems having worked previously for global organizations in this sector. David and Alan set themselves a first-year turnover target of £4 million and are well on course to double this projection. Shortly after the launch of the business, the duo were joined by Bernie Kersh, who took up the position of Sales Director.

David and Alan source products worldwide to ensure they can secure the best possible price for customers. All products are manufactured by major IT companies such as IBM, HP, Cisco and Sun Micro Systems. ITHS sells its products to national IT distributors and large corporate organizations.

The business employs eight people and is based on Mount Heath Trading Estate in Prestwich. David and Alan have plans to recruit an additional two new employees in the next few weeks as the business continues to grow.

David Warner, Managing Director of ITHS, said:

We launched ITHS because we believed there was a gap in the market for a fast and knowledgeable IT sourcing business in the North West. Our approach of providing clients with quick, cost-effective solutions has been well received by the market. We are very pleased with our initial performance and are confident of further growth in turnover as the business becomes more established.

Jo Jones, Relationship Manager for RBSIF added:

David, Alan and Bernie have a wealth of experience in this sector and have used this to good effect to launch ITHS. Their success is impressive given the challenging economic environment and we look forward to watching the company's future development.

Case Study 2 – RBS Backs MiddletonMurray with Invoice Finance solution

RBS has supported recruitment company MiddletonMurray Recruitment Solutions (MMRS) with a new invoice finance line that converts their invoices into cash.

MMRS is the brainchild of entrepreneur Angela Middleton. Having worked at BP Oil and The Woolwich for 17 years and then left in 2001 to spend time with her children, Angela decided to set up her own business that would give her the flexibility she was looking for as a mother. During her time at BP and Woolwich, Angela had valuable exposure to the recruitment sector by employing several consultants, and soon after starting the business in 2002 she employed her sister-in-law, Lisa Murray, who had 10 years' experience as a recruitment consultant, as Director. MMRS covers a wide range of sectors including education, IT, accountancy and building to name but a few. Over the past couple of years, Angela noticed an increase in contract business and looked for a bank that could find a working capital solution to help the business respond to this change. Richard Hanson at RBS Invoice Finance was happy to put together a finance package that included the invoice finance line.

Angela Middleton, Owner and Managing Director at MMRS, said:

> We have responded to the changing market and worked with RBS to put in place the invoice finance arrangement which effectively allows us to turn our invoices into cash, releasing working capital for further growth. The new arrangement works well for us and we're thankful to Richard Hanson at RBS Invoice Finance for finding us a flexible solution and putting it in place so quickly.

Richard Hanson, Business Development Manager, RBS Invoice Finance, added:

> Although the recruitment sector generally has suffered due to the current economic climate, MMRS are bucking the trend thanks to their wide sector spread and strong management team. They have enjoyed consistent turnover and profit levels over the years and because they've adapted their business plan, this is set to continue. Invoice finance is a particularly good fit for recruitment companies and MMRS is an excellent example of how it can help during these difficult times.

Case Study 3 – Temporary Staff Agency Announces Latest Acquisition with NatWest Support

South East recruitment agency, Kent Staff Services 2000 Ltd, has established itself as the largest supplier of temporary staff in the South East of England following the purchase of an additional recruitment agency, thanks to funding from NatWest.

Established in Kent in the 1990s, Kent Staff is an independently owned company specializing in the recruitment of skilled and unskilled labour to a wide range of industrial businesses. Operating from Gravesend, Hastings and Folkestone, the company was looking to expand their regional remit and has since acquired Storm Personnel Services Ltd, based in Dunstable, taking on four new clients, bringing a combined annual turnover of £3 million. Kent Staff has grown the business considerably from £1 million to an impressive £15 million turnover to date. In addition, Kent Staff employs 1,300 staff, 200 of whom have been retained from Dunstable.

Thanet Earth is the company's latest business win, and Kent Staff is providing packers to assist with the distribution of eco-friendly vegetables to supermarkets. The state-of-the-art greenhouse development, based on the Isle of Thanet, is the largest greenhouse complex in the United Kingdom and a positive acquisition for Kent Staff.

Following a nine-year relationship with NatWest, Paul Kidd, Managing Director of Kent Staff approached NatWest for support with their expansion plans. Stuart Furlong, Relationship Manager at NatWest, and his colleague Rob McGarvey, RBS Invoice Finance Manager, worked closely to provide an invoice discounting facility to fund working capital. This will allow for Kent Staff to acquire their new Dunstable-based operation as well as taking on additional headcount to manage their new clients.

This latest finance package derives from the NatWest and RBS SME Regional Fund, which sees an additional £250 million funding available to SMEs in the South East in 2009, demonstrating its commitment to the government in supporting this sector.

Paul Kidd, MD of Kent Staff Services 2000 Ltd, commented:

This is an exciting time for the business as we expand regionally and employ additional staff, which we see as a positive move in this difficult climate. We look forward to forming close relationships with our new clients and continuing to provide our existing clients with a high calibre of temporary staff. I am grateful to NatWest for supporting us on our latest phase of expansion.

Do you have the courage to establish cash-generating behaviours in your business?

Niall Cooter, PricewaterhouseCoopers

What does good look like?

We all know that Cash is King, but what does that actually mean and what are the behaviours that drive that ethos? More significantly, how do we establish those behaviours across a business with a diverse set of functional objectives, not to mention the varying capabilities and personality types that may exist within the business?

When we think of high-performing organizations, it conjures up images of a dynamic group of people working to a common goal. These individuals will typically display high levels of tenacity and drive; they will be comfortable operating both within the detail and at a more strategic level. But above all, the high-performing team will have a clear focus on an endgame and they will each understand how they personally contribute to the achievement of that objective. And it remains true that what gets measured gets done. When this measurement is accompanied by an incentivization scheme, it gets done quicker.

What behaviours do we see in underperforming companies?

Underperforming companies often exhibit some of the worst behaviours. Often it is these behaviours that have resulted in the organization's current predicament. However, instead of management taking decisive action to address these behaviours, the behaviours can become ever more entrenched; silo walls become higher, the politics of business grows fat on the excessive diet of blame and mistrust.

Often, management seem either unwilling or unable to act. Do they not see these behaviours for what they are? Do they feel powerless to address them? Or are they as entrenched in these behaviours as the rest of the organization? In many cases, management do see these insidious behaviours and do try to address them; often with limited success. So this raises the question. 'How do you drive the right behaviours?' A simple question, surely? It is just about managing the team effectively; up-skilling them, effective measurement and reward systems, effective communications, isn't it? But there are countless examples of best intentions not working:

- One Chief Executive, concerned at the level of invoicing errors, decided to penalize any sales person who raised more than three credit notes in a month. Clearly the desire was to improve the quality of order acceptance and invoicing. Instead, Sales stopped issuing credit notes once they had hit their limit of three; there was no change in the quality of order processing!
- One Director determined that the secret to improving collection performance was to improve the work rate of the credit team. Targets were set and bonuses paid based on the number of cases closed. As a consequence, the easier, low-value cases were prioritized. The result was poor cash collections as higher-value cases remained unsettled.

The reason for such failed initiatives varies but tends to fall into one or more of the following categories:

- Conflicting objectives – failing to establish shared objectives across a value chain (eg sales to cash) or not making connections across value chains. The end result is quite often an entrenchment of functional divides or silos.
- Outcome obsessed – focusing on the desired behaviour without taking care to understand what drives the current undesirable behaviours. This can lead to incentives that have no chance of delivering the intended behaviours. We must try to understand why individuals exhibit certain behaviours if we wish to change those behaviours.
- Unconsidered solutions – acting instinctively without asking the question 'What is the worst that could happen if I do this?'. This can result in undesirable behaviours that do not facilitate the business objective.

Where do these undesirable behaviours come from?

To understand where behaviours come from, we need to look further than the personalities of the individuals concerned. We need to look at the organization holistically.

If we take the concept of Team and break that down, we start to see the emergence of one possible cause. A team could be defined as 'a group of people working to a common goal'. But what is that goal? Is it clearly defined? Is it really a 'common goal'? Take the sales to cash process and consider these 'common goals':

- To maximize profitable sales – a good start! The business is aligned with the objective of maximizing sales, minimizing dilutions and reducing bad debts. But what of maximizing cash and improving efficiency; where do they come in?
- To maximize earnings before interest and tax (EBIT) – again, where does cash come in? Interest saved on borrowings comes below the EBIT line.
- To ensure that customers' invoices are paid on time – now we are talking. But hang on, how do sales people relate to that? As a salesman, do I need to start chasing debts? Do I turn down profitable sales because the customer wants extended payment terms?

In many businesses the overall objective will often be to maximize sales or margin. But typically each function within the business will have its own specific objective or reason for being. In many sales-driven businesses, for example, the role of Finance is to look after the money and let sales and operations do the core business activity. The result is functional objectives that are not necessarily aligned or linked in any way. And this can breed undesirable behaviours.

And the danger of creating apparently conflicting objectives across a value chain is that those individual goals create individual teams; we have now created a differentiator or divide between groups of people. Rather than one team across a business or value chain you have several teams. In essence you have created a competitive environment where each team is striving to outwit and outperform the others, but not necessarily to the benefit of the business as a whole.

How do we change behaviour?

The solution is to establish a link between apparently conflicting objectives to create one shared objective, ideally, throughout the organization. Consider the objective that 'we will maximize the quantum of our cash position'. On the face of it, this is a traditional Finance department objective. But think about the linkage across value chains:

- Sales will continue to pursue sales in the knowledge that more sales equals more cash – but only if sufficient care is taken to ensure that cash is not wasted due to increased costs associated with rework or bad debts. Furthermore, they will be acutely aware that longer payment terms reduce cash in real terms but also increase the exposure to bad debts.

- Production will be encouraged to pursue cost-efficient production schedules whilst optimizing stock holdings.
- Purchasing will drive for the best price with the best payment terms but will guard against deals that result in increased rework costs or increased stock-holding requirements.
- Infrastructure, IT and HR will be encouraged not only to provide the infrastructure required for the business to meet its objectives, but it will also be encouraged to reduce the costs of the services it provides. For example, when we start to challenge how we use our real estate we can uncover opportunities to reduce or reclaim business rates from under-utilized space.
- Finance (accounting, treasury and tax) can undertake a role that not only tracks the finances but is also challenged to look at how they contribute to cash. For example, have we fully explored opportunities to delay or reduce the tax cash outflow of the business?
- Payables and Receivables are driven not only to maximize the cash position but also to strive to reduce the costs involved. But more than this, we might also expect to see a more commercial attitude to credit risk for example.

Clearly, these functions are still focusing on the things that have always been important to them, but, by finding the linkages to a common objective, in this case 'maximizing the quantum of cash', we establish the common bond between turnover, margin and cash. In reading this, we might expect a good number of executives to say, 'Yep, we have many of those behaviours in our organization', and expect to receive a pat on the back for doing so. But before that, consider this: to what extent are we displaying these behaviours and, even more fundamentally, if you can't tick all the boxes, can you really say that the business is fully aligned to a common objective?

Now that we have identified a common objective, the hard part starts. How do we embed this objective within the business and what do we need to do differently in order to establish behaviours consistent with our objective?

The key to changing the behaviour of individuals is to ensure that they understand and trust in both the objective and the behavioural change required. For example, will an employee truly believe in the business's cost-cutting drive if the Chief Executive continues to fly first class? Essentially, the objective and behavioural change required must not only be preached from above but must also be undeniably exhibited from the Chief Executive downwards. This will be clear from the messages and communications to the business but also in the measurement and reward systems implemented. You need reward systems that reflect the shared objectives and reward behaviours that are consistent with the objective and penalize those that are not.

But again we must guard against complacency here. The moment we think that this is easy, or the answer is obvious, we miss some key component and everything goes horribly wrong. In the book, *Freakonomics*, the authors Stephen Dubner and Steven Levitt discussed how a childcare provider introduced a financial penalty for the late collection of children. Unfortunately, not only did this fail to encourage prompt collection; it actually resulted in an increased incidence of late collection. This happened because the organizers assumed that a financial penalty would be an adequate incentive; instead, it established a mindset in the parents that extended childcare was available at a cost and as such they did not need to feel that parental guilt they had previously associated with a late collection.

What are we hoping to see from this change?

A business that adopts this common objective and establishes the appropriate, desired behaviours will expect to establish the type of culture associated with the best-performing businesses. We could define an extensive list of attributes including the words tenacity, drive, commitment and teamwork. However, when we take a more strategic view of the business we would expect to see:

■ Cash is at the heart of the business. Sales retain the drive to maximize sales and margin but have also bought into the finance mantra that 'a sale is not a sale until it is paid for'. Credit Control take it as a personal affront if payment is made late and leave no stone unturned in their efforts to secure prompt payment of all monies due, while the rest of the business visualize the cash impact of their actions whether it be the costs they incur or inefficient processes.

■ A keen eye on cost optimization and control. But this is not the radical slashing of costs for the sake of saving money. This is a pragmatic attitude to incurring cost that is demonstrated at all the levels of the business. Individuals are aware that any cost in the business needs to make a return and the greater that return the better. This can extend to the management of credit risk and bad debts. For example, a haulier business that is expecting an empty lorry on a return leg might sell that space to a high-risk customer on the basis of (say) 40 per cent payment in advance and the remaining 60 per cent on credit terms. It is true that the 60 per cent is at risk; however, the 40 per cent is almost entirely profit in a scenario where the return leg would have been a 100 per cent cost to the business. The remaining 60 per cent has no cost attached to it; therefore, we have lost nothing if the debt becomes bad.

■ An unerring focus on customer satisfaction and quality. We will see cross-functional working parties addressing the underlying cause of error and inefficiency. The business lives by the ethos of continuous improvement; effectively there is always an opportunity to do better. For example, the business will not be happy at having the lowest days sales outstanding (DSO) or the greatest margin and market share in the industry. The business will be constantly looking for opportunities to improve margin and cash.

Whilst these could be seen as potentially conflicting behaviours, in the high-performing business they are likely to be linked by, for example, their relationship to cash. The high-performing business will ensure that these behaviours exist in perfect balance. The risk, if this balance is lost, is that one of those behaviours will be dominant at the expense of the rest. If this happens, the business is unlikely to achieve its full potential and may be more susceptible to changing economic and market conditions.

Do you have the courage to make change happen?

One of the most common obstacles to change is Executive inaction. This is typically due to ignorance of the issue or denial, which often materializes as a refusal to accept responsibility for delivering change. Denial is one of the most common reasons that we encounter for inaction and for which there are many underlying reasons:

■ One Finance Director that we worked with agreed with our assessment that debtors could be reduced by changing business practices and behaviours. He also agreed with our assessment that this could release £27 million of cash during the course of the next financial year. However, his reason for doing nothing was that he was not under pressure to deliver any working capital improvements.

■ Another Finance Director was concerned that the existence of opportunity within his area of control, working capital, would result in him attracting criticism from his peers; the greater the opportunity, the greater the criticism. In this situation, the Finance Director may choose to quickly usher us out of the door and hope that no one notices the opportunity.

These are just two examples, amongst many, where decisions to act have been deferred because the business leaders have lacked the courage or vision to stand up and make a difference.

Let's consider that last example again. There is an alternative solution that demonstrates not only courage but also an understanding that whilst the management of cash may lie within Finance it is the behaviours and working practices across an organization that determine its quantum. In this case, that Finance Director might choose to embrace the challenge and take responsibility for tackling the underling causes, many of which are outside of his direct control.

The challenge to all executives is this: 'Do you have the courage to make change happen?'

AMRIL ™

credit management specialists

Increase cash flow...

Cash flow is the lifeblood of business.

We at Amril understand this and have experience in working with clients to achieve a healthy cash flow.

We can help your business with:

- Credit management.
- Business recovery.
- Invoice collection.
- Outsourcing.
- Training.

"It's not Credit Management, it's Relationship Management"

Web: Amril.co.uk
Email: Enquiries@Amril.co.uk
Phone: 01903 215748

National debt (business to business) UK

Graham D Sands, Amril Limited

Every business knows the services or products they are trading in, but not all businesses know how to deal with cash flow. Cash flow is the vital bloodline to the heart of your business; if this fails, your business fails. That is the harsh reality.

In this chapter I hope to give you an understanding of how to control your sales ledger and reduce your Debtor Sales Outstanding (DSO): in other words ensuring that you are being paid on your contractual terms. We have all heard the saying 'cash is king', and in this difficult environment, it is vital that your business understands the fundamentals of running a small or large credit control function to reduce your DSO, which in turn will increase your cash flow and reduce interest payments on any overdraft facility you might be using.

Cash flow and its importance

In the twelve months ending 31 March 2009, approximately 1 in 120 active UK companies, or 0.8 per cent, went into liquidation.

Additionally, there were 1,529 other corporate insolvencies in the second quarter of 2009 (not seasonally adjusted), comprising 345 receiverships, 1,027 administrations and 157 company voluntary arrangements. In total these represented an increase of 22.7 per cent on the same period the previous year.

Controlling your cash flow is so important not only for the reason I have mentioned but, for example, when you require an additional injection of funds to buy new equipment or launch a new product line. If investors see that your cash flow is strong and your clients are paying you on time, they are more likely to invest.

Allowing debtors to double your payment terms shows an investor you are not managing the clients you already have, and it will therefore consider you a higher risk and could decline the offer to invest, whether it be a bank or a private investor.

There is a strong chance, depending on the industry you are in, that 40 to 45 per cent of your customer base will probably pay you late, but you don't have to be a statistic in the late payment culture if you put in place simple credit control procedures and are disciplined in your actions.

Most businesses have delayed payment of an invoice at some point, often past the due date. It is very tempting to do this, especially if your sales are down and there are no consequences for paying late. What all businesses need to realize is that even if you are small, your payment history is being tracked and reported on, and that information is passed to other businesses for evaluation.

So with this in mind, look at where a substantial amount of cash may be tied up on your sales ledger, otherwise known as account receivables or debtors. All successful businesses rely on money flowing through the company at a certain rate to meet business commitments. If this flow of money is sluggish, then you have a cash-flow issue.

Credit control

Effective credit control doesn't just happen; it is the result of careful planning.

Credit control is not an exact science. It takes dedication, hard work and discipline to set up and maintain a credit control function in line with your business commitments and future operations.

So, you have built up a client base and you are finding out that your business could do more to control your sales ledger. Your debtor days are getting out of control and procedures have not been properly adjusted to address the business environment in which we find ourselves now, as opposed to two years ago when credit was easy to come by.

Customer credit status

Let's say for argument's sake you have not thoroughly checked your customer's credit worthiness. If this is the case, do it now. Credit check every company you deal with, regardless of whether they are a long-term customer or not; any business in any environment can suffer a cash-flow crisis.

There are reputable organizations that can assist with credit checking and the monitoring of your client base, and this action needs to be taken seriously to avoid the traps that the unwary fall into. Look at the industry spread you have. Are there customers in a particular industry that control a large percentage of your sales ledger? If so, consider spreading the risk in case a large debtor falls into arrears. What would be the worst-case scenario for your cash flow? What actions could you take to reduce that risk?

The risk of fraud

Another issue that needs to be considered is the high potential of fraud, which cannot be taken lightly. It is vital to know your customer in order to prevent or reduce the risk of fraud externally.

According to KPMG's Fraud Barometer, over 160 cases of serious fraud with charges over £100,000 worth a total value of £636 million came to UK courts in the first half of 2009. This is the highest number of cases in a six-month period throughout the 21-year history of the Barometer (The Fraud Advisory Panel).

The Fraud Act 2006 came into effect on 15 January 2007. The Act creates a new general offence of fraud with three categories:

■ fraud by false representation;
■ fraud by failing to disclose information; and
■ fraud by abuse of position.

Coping with the consequences of even minor fraud will consume management time, which is already at a premium, especially with the current UK economy.

In addition, you should minimize the opportunities for fraud to occur within your business. Review your business activities, identify the areas most at risk to fraud and introduce controls to prevent it.

Regular credit checks

So, as explained, credit check all your current customers and make this a regular review, say, every six months. You may even decide to monitor a few that you feel concerned about; that way you will know in an effective time frame if your customer is in trouble and will be in a position to act. This will help you understand the environment that your sales team are investigating and will help control potential bad debt and fraud.

Personal relationships

The next consideration is the members of staff who find it very difficult to speak to the customer about payments or overdue invoicing. My advice would be to move them to a more appropriate job role. Credit Control is not for everyone and as an organization we are encountering this phenomenon more and more. This one factor alone could reduce your cash-flow targets. Utilize staff that love to talk and are analytical, but ensure that they keep to the topic of concern.

Being personal is a very good thing; people love to chat. You would be amazed at how much information relating to their business can be gathered by being friendly and polite. Make it an objective to have a good relationship with two people in the Accounts Department. They are the people that will put you on the payment run either this week or next month. I once worked with a very large organization who agreed to pay on the 60-day contractual terms, but as a result of developing a positive relationship with this company, the Accounts Department paid on 30 days.

Always try to send an invoice within a few days of the sale. Ring the customer to ensure that they have received the invoice and are in agreement with all aspects, to avoid later disputes. Ring again a week later to confirm that the Accounts Department has the invoice and that it has been signed off. Also establish when their payment dates are each month and when you will be paid. Agree a date.

Never be afraid to ask a customer whether they have cash-flow problems. They will never divulge this independently until it is too late. If you believe something is amiss, discuss your concerns and see if there is anything that you as an organization can do to assist.

I cannot stress highly enough how important your relationship is with your customer. If you are able to offer a payment plan with clear action points, you have a stronger chance of keeping that customer and acquiring further business.

Look for the danger signs when dealing with your customers, such as erratic patterns of payment, difficulty in contacting key individuals or a marked change in staff, an increase in complaints or credit lines being exceeded.

The roles of staff and management

The sales team

Use your sales team. They are an invaluable tool and an integral part of the process in confirming your customer's status. Never consider them as 'just another department' or that they are only interested in completing a sale. I can assure you that they will not want to spend time on a customer that cannot sustain a credit limit. They are in regular face-to-face contact with the customer and are well placed to influence decisions, especially those regarding disputes over invoices. Encourage and guide them to think outside the 'sales box'.

Draw up a document for the sales team so that they know the type of questions that need to be asked. They may not get all the answers you want but they will get a feel for the company and how smoothly it runs.

Make sure the sales team get information on the Purchase Order (PO) System if required. This alone will help to accelerate payments. Get the correct contacts and understand the processes of authorization to receive accurate details and amounts on the PO.

Your sales team are in a prime position to ask general questions, such as how long their potential customer has been at the premises, whether they own or rent the premises and how many staff they have. Establish which other suppliers they use and pass those details to the credit team to investigate. Instruct a member of your sales team to conduct a tour of the premises in order to gauge how the business gels with its employees and always consider your own trading experience and seek opinions from other companies who may have done business with your potential client.

The credit management team

None of the above is a time-wasting exercise. Any business can complete a form giving two trade references, which will reveal nothing, as no company large or small is going to direct you to companies where their payment performance is poor. Do not just rely on your reference sheet or the credit report for essential information as this is only a snapshot of the business. You may say to yourself that you and your team have no time for this, but never forget that you are looking for long-term relationships. Repeat business is far cheaper to maintain and reduces your chances of having bad debt on your books.

If you have concerns regarding a company's credit report, request a copy of the updated Management Accounts, explaining your reasoning and assuring them that all information will be kept strictly confidential. They may refuse, but it is definitely worth asking. Always consider speaking to the customer face to face. You will achieve better results by doing this and you might be in a position to gain further sales. In business we all want to make money and you may decide that the potential customer's value is worth the risk. If this is the case you may consider agreeing on reduced payment terms of 14 days for the first three months, or cash upfront. If possible arrange a meeting to discuss this in detail.

Dealing with large corporations

If you are going to deal with large organizations, you may have to accept their terms and conditions. You might want the sale, but make sure your cash flow can support 60 day plus payment terms.

There are large companies that have outsourced their Accounts Payable team abroad, say to India, and this alone can be very time-consuming and frustrating. Try to make contact with the Accounts Payable Manager and request one of their team members to deal with you directly in order to avoid confusion and the possibility of delayed payment.

The credit control function is not an exact science, so you need to use all the tools available to you to reduce the chances of bad debt.

Payment practices

Payment practices have changed drastically within this last year alone and, according to Atradius, credit periods are being extended. Before September 2008, almost 80 per cent of businesses rated their customer payment performance as good, very good or excellent.

By March 2009, 50 per cent ranked customer payments as poor or mediocre. The frequency of payment defaults has risen by over 140 per cent, with businesses reporting a higher incidence of non-payment.

Credit control

When it comes to record keeping, always keep a log of the calls made: who you spoke to, what was stated and when. Log the customer's payment dates on your system and always get the details of the person in charge of the accounts team, so that if you have concerns about payment issues you can contact them directly.

Instruct your credit controllers to write a monthly cash-flow forecast, stating when in the month payment will be received, and, if not received, get them to chase immediately. Be direct in asking why the payment has not arrived; after all it is your money.

Pre-empting litigation

Litigation should be the last thing on anyone's mind. There are far better ways of dealing with situations that come to a head, such as payment plans or goods being withheld until a satisfactory conclusion can be reached.

Invite the customer to your premises, or better still arrange a meeting at theirs so that you can discuss a way forward. By doing this you will strengthen your relationship, if it's not already too late.

Be sure to consider another point regarding record keeping. If you have kept a complete record of all conversations made, including dates and times, this will assist you down the litigation route, but careful planning and proper procedures will reduce the need for litigation and will also significantly reduce your bad debt.

Sales ledger insurance

I won't talk a great deal about insuring your Sales Ledger, but be aware before you contemplate this course of action that it is imperative to get your accounts department in shape. Insurers will want to know your annual turnover, any bad debt issues, what procedures you have in place including the granting of credit limits, on what basis you gave your customer the credit limit in the first place and how often they go over the limit. They will also want to look at the spread of customers against the industries you are selling to in relation to your turnover. If you have concerns about your sales ledger, see what is out there and always be prepared to shop around.

Terms and conditions

One last thing before I close, let's talk briefly about your Terms and Conditions of Sale (T & Cs); always get professional legal advice when writing the T & Cs. Don't ever consider doing them yourself and always get a signature from the customer before any transactions take place. Attach your T & Cs to the back of your invoicing and include the Late Payment Act. You may never use it, but it is a good negotiating tool and it shows that your company understands its rights.

If you have a late payment issue, contact the customer and point out that this Act can be utilized if payments are not strictly brought back up to date and assurances are received that this will be the case. Always monitor closely to ensure that this occurs. If the customer reneges on this commitment, you will need to decide how to proceed in line with the Late Payment Act.

If at all possible avoid 'Purchase Agreements' as this could override your own T & Cs. Always include a 'Retention of Title' (RoT). This will simplify the recovery of goods if the buyer goes insolvent or for non-payment. Make sure your credit policy is also in line with your T & Cs.

Hopefully, you and your organization will benefit from this summary of my experience. I wish you the very best of luck.

Paying on time is good for business – the prompt payment code

Philip King, The Institute of Credit Management

For too long there has been a tacit understanding that the idea of 'late payment' is acceptable.

A report in the summer of 2009, for example, from one of the big finance houses suggested that more than two million small businesses were struggling from the pressures of late payment, and that the 'ripple effect' (in particular the effect that late payment has on supplies) could be costing UK businesses as much as £2 billion a year.

The British Government itself published statistics at the end of 2009 that suggested payments between businesses in the UK are typically made 20 or more days beyond agreed terms, and that overdue payments over the same year will cost British businesses £180 million on debt interest charges alone. Whatever research you choose to read, or whatever figures you decide to accept, the issue of late payment is a big one.

Larger companies, in particular, believe they have the right to extended credit terms – terms that are sometimes extended still further without agreement, negotiation or redress. They have done so and continue to do so because they can; because despite there being legislation that gives suppliers the right to charge interest on late payment, they almost never do. Small businesses especially are too frightened that the buyer will simply find a new supplier.

In an age of corporate social responsibility (CSR), this is a huge irony: big companies are quick to promote their CSR credentials and seize both the moral and ethical high ground as a means of gaining competitive advantage. But how many, if any, have 'prompt payment' as part of their CSR statement? And how many list 'suppliers' as being important 'stakeholders'?

It is against this very background that the department for Business Enterprise and Regulatory Reform (BERR), since renamed the department for Business, Innovation and Skills (BIS), opted to advance the late payment debate in the winter of 2008/09, initially by producing a series of *Managing Cashflow Guides* in conjunction with the Institute of Credit Management (ICM). Within these guides, the very specific issue of 'late payment' was addressed and prompted a wider discussion around the launch of a Prompt Payment Code.

Giving life to the code was not as simple as it might have sounded. First it meant getting over some of the (many) misconceptions – many of them within the BIS itself. There was a desire, early in its development, that the code should demand a blanket '30 day' payment term. However, this was destined to fail from the start since it would stifle business rather than encouraging it. It also failed to acknowledge how some businesses take the opportunity of reduced payment for early settlement, or vary product delivery or volumes based on the credit available.

Where such prescriptive doctrines fundamentally missed the point was in failing to consider what terms may be 'fair' or 'appropriate'. A farmer providing milk to a supermarket might accept credit terms of seven days, whereas a manufacturer of aero engines might not think 12-months' credit unreasonable.

With those issues addressed, and the arguments won, the Prompt Payment Code was finally launched in the early part of 2009 and, within a few months, more than 600 businesses, government departments and local authorities had signed up to the code and a further 35,000 enterprises had taken advantage of the free health checks. But there is still more to be done to convince businesses as to the benefits of paying suppliers on time.

The code, which enjoys the support of nearly all of the major business organizations, aims to establish a clear and consistent policy in the payment of business-to-business invoices. It is a simple statement of policy and a commitment between a customer and its suppliers. In it, a customer agrees to:

■ pay suppliers on time
  – within the terms agreed at the outset of the contract,
  – without attempting to change payment terms retrospectively,
  – without changing practice on length of payment for smaller companies on unreasonable grounds;
■ give clear guidance to suppliers
  – providing suppliers with clear and easily accessible guidance on payment procedures,

     – ensuring that there is a system for dealing with complaints and disputes which is communicated to suppliers,
     – advising them promptly if there is any reason why an invoice will not be paid to the agreed terms;
■ Encourage good practice
     – by requesting that lead suppliers encourage adoption of the code throughout their own supply chains.

At a time when money is tight and cash flow critical, it may sound counter-intuitive to some to be encouraging buyers within business or local government to part with their money more quickly in order to pay suppliers. However, the advantages go far deeper than simply being seen to treat your customers more fairly. There can be real financial benefits.

In the same way that every supplier wants to be the 'preferred' party, so too do buyers want to be first on their suppliers' list. Prompt payment acts towards establishing the very best customer–supplier relationships, which in turn enables customers to negotiate better deals and avoid such issues as late payment interest charges.

Furthermore, when perception is everything, it delivers a signal to the market of confidence and sound financial well-being that in turn promotes further mutual business opportunities and growth.

The response to the code has been most encouraging. Within the government departments that were among the first to 'sign up' were the:

■ Department for Children, Schools and Families;
■ Department for Communities and Local Government;
■ Department for Culture, Media and Sport;
■ Department for Innovation, Universities and Skills;
■ Department for International Development;
■ Department for Transport;
■ Department of Health; and
■ Department for Work and Pensions

They have been joined by a raft of different government agencies, NGOs and trade associations such as HM Treasury, HM Revenue and Customs, the East Midlands Development Agency, the Northwest Regional Development Agency, the FPB, FSB and IoD. And, arguably of most note within the media, are the major corporates including BAE Systems, British Gas Business, John Lewis PLC, and Lloyds TSB which have also committed themselves to the Prompt Payment Code.

The thoughts of just a handful reflect the thinking behind the campaign. Stuart Hopewell, Credit Manager, FujiFilm UK Limited says that 'prompt payment can actually result in reduced costs for both debtor and creditor, and increase profitability'.

Monica Turner, Financial Controller of ASDA agrees:

> The code absolutely fits our philosophy of saving money every day. Paying suppliers on time means we cut out unnecessary costs from the supply chain which ensures we

deliver low prices and good availability to our customers. We try and live the code by making our payment processes transparent to suppliers through our 'Where's My Invoice' facility. Through this we provide suppliers a view of their account and a way of resolving discrepancies between us and their accounts.

We recognise these are difficult times, particularly for our small suppliers and as a result we have strengthened our query resolution resource for small suppliers.

Robert McTiffin, Managing Director, Nationwide Property Solutions Limited, also recognizes that difficult times lie ahead, but that protecting supplier relationships is key:

By paying all our subcontractors at agreed terms, we maintain our own integrity and get priority service. By guaranteeing prompt payment, the best subcontractors want to work for us. Paying on time means that suppliers will do more for the same price; subcontractors will put themselves out for us; we receive referrals and recommendations as a preferred client; and we don't waste time responding to payment enquiries. In short, everyone wins.

Paul Bennett, Head of Purchase to Pay Solutions, BBC, shares a similar view:

To ensure strong commercial relationships it is essential that suppliers know when they can expect to be paid and understand any circumstances which may cause delay in payment. Through our website – Supplying the BBC – and deployment of e-tools we are increasing visibility of the payment process to our suppliers.

The code is working because it focuses on three main areas that anyone involved in credit understands: a commitment to pay suppliers on time; to give clear guidance to suppliers; and to encourage good practice.

But perhaps, just perhaps, a formal code is not quite enough. If the government and British industry are really serious about protecting the SME community and serious about enterprise, then change has to come from the top. It has to lead, and big businesses should follow.

Smaller businesses are often afraid to ask for better terms because they are frightened of losing the business, when in fact they should be confident in the service that they provide, and not simply take on new business because it is a 'big name' with an impressive logo for their website to show them in good company. Bad business is bad business, regardless of the name.

Actually, what there needs to be in business is a new moral code – a code that says it is inherently wrong to keep a supplier waiting for payment.

The Prompt Payment Code is hosted by the ICM on a dedicated website (www. promptpaymentcode.org.uk) and includes a facility for suppliers to raise concerns about late payers. Advice on managing cash flow is available at www.creditmanagement.org.uk/managingcashflowguide.htm.

Part 2

Improving cash flow

Our 3-in-1 credit report is a real winner

Graydon can address all three of your key credit management concerns in ONE report - something you can't get from any other source. Our Level 3 report can predict whether you will be paid on time, whether a business is likely to fail and can detect unusual business behaviour that may indicate possible fraud. This winning combination means you need look no further when making key business decisions, saving you valuable time and resource.

Does your current credit agency provide you with this level of information? If not, give Graydon a call today. Call us on 020 8515 1410 or email mail@graydon.co.uk quoting 'Level 3 report'

Preventing slow payments: do not suffer in silence

Martin Williams, Graydon UK Ltd

No matter what size your business is, a sale is only a sale when the invoice is paid. Cash flow is an essential ingredient for business continuity and success, so it is vital that a business does everything it can to collect cash from customers on time.

Since it is estimated that around half of all UK trade invoices are paid late, it is fair to assume that most businesses will experience issues relating to delayed payments from clients. This perennial problem has been exacerbated still further by the current credit crunch. Not only do we all have a problem with those companies that are unwilling to pay; we also have a serious and growing problem with customers who cannot pay because of their poor financial condition. Unfortunately, it's also true that smaller businesses will probably suffer most from this 'delayed payment' affliction. That's because many bigger organizations 'bully' smaller suppliers into accepting slower payments or demanding discounts for prompt payment, in the knowledge that the smaller supplier is so grateful for the business that it will turn a blind eye to tardy invoice settlements or unwarranted demands. Secondly, most growing companies cannot afford to employ a professional credit manager, who would normally have a range of tricks and skills to get the cash in on time.

It's not all gloom and doom, however. If you are a small and growing business, a number of positive steps can be taken to minimize the impact of late payments, even avoid them altogether, without going to the expense of hiring a credit management professional.

General principles

First, the law is on your side! The Late Payment of Commercial Debts (Interest) Act of 1998 gives small businesses the right to charge debtors interest on overdue payments. The large majority of small businesses are worried about pushing for this right for fear of upsetting/losing the customer, but in the southwest of England, a recent survey suggested that as many as 29 per cent of businesses regularly added interest to overdue invoices. So maybe they're a little braver in the West Country than most.

Please recognize that cash flow is the lifeblood of your business – don't just take excuses for delayed payments with a submissive acceptance speech. The British in particular can be too darned polite and accommodating in these situations; like being too reticent in complaining about poor food or service in restaurants. Anything but make a fuss, eh!

Take note: any perceived lack of interest or urgency by a supplier in getting paid will be seen as weakness by the slow payer, and that would mean your outstanding invoice going to the bottom of the finance department's in-tray. So be polite but assertive in asking for what you want.

Secondly, spread your risk. As a small business, be careful about having too many eggs in one basket with regards to commercial trade debt. There are countless tales of smaller companies going to the wall because a large customer accounting for a disproportionate amount of sales turnover did not pay up on time. Pareto's Law is a good indicator as to what customer mix should be aimed for (80 per cent of turnover should come from the top 20 per cent of your client base).

How to improve cash collection

Here are 10 more ways to improve cash collection.

1. Sign your customer up

Ensure your company has got a signed contract with the customer that clearly states your payment terms. These terms should also be clearly described on your application forms and the invoices you subsequently send out. Be sure they know what the credit terms are, whether you offer discounts for prompt payments or bulk purchases, whether additional costs are payable (eg VAT or carriage costs), and whether you charge interest on overdue accounts (all businesses are legally entitled to do this). If a customer tries to unilaterally impose its payment terms on you, make sure you build that additional cost of extended credit into your prices so that your profits aren't marginalized further.

2. Do a credit check

Buy a credit report from a recognized credit reference agency; especially one that collects trade payment information on how large companies pay their bills, eg Graydon, Experian, and Dun and Bradstreet. Don't rely totally on the taking up of two references given to you by the potential client. They may be cultivated. Don't be taken in either by a great-looking set of accounts to determine whether you will get paid on time; a healthy-looking balance sheet might mean that your potential customer is very proficient in getting its suppliers to finance its business. Set a credit limit for each new client, and don't allow customers to exceed limits without your permission. After all, they are set for a good reason, as you have assessed the creditworthiness of the customer and how much your business can afford to wait for (or lose, should the worst scenario occur).

3. Is a purchase order required?

As part of their internal control procedures, large companies often require signed purchase orders before paying invoices. Ask the manager/department placing the order whether they need to raise an internal PO, and if so, have they done so, covering the value of the order. Ask for a copy of the PO (NB: some large companies require invoices from suppliers to quote the PO number before they are paid).

4. Prevent excuses

Prevent excuses for delayed payment – after dispatching goods and sending your invoice quickly afterwards, make a pre-due call to ensure that your customer has received them and that there are no problems with quantity or quality of the goods supplied, or with the content of the invoice. Invoice disputes can be very genuine and can push back the time you get paid by weeks or even months sometimes.

5. Send statements

Send statements at different times in the month from your invoices. Sometimes this tactic can provoke questions, particularly when original invoices have been lost, not received, or mislaid.

6. Check on expected pay date

Confirm with your client when your bill is expected to be paid, remembering to ask whether they have specific cheque-run dates.

7. Use the telephone (or even a personal visit) to chase

If payment is delayed, chase your money by telephone rather than letter. Some experts in this field say that the telephone method can be 80 per cent more effective. Always prioritize your cash collection activity, making sure you chase the oldest and largest debts first. Be friendly but firm when speaking with them, and don't forget to remind them that you could charge interest on all late payments. If it's a big debt, don't dismiss the idea of turning up on the doorstep and waiting for your cheque. It does work! I know of one woman who runs a small recruitment agency in Watford. She always suffers from delayed payments from her largest client – a corporation that's financially robust if a little tardy on payments to non-crucial suppliers. Every so often, when her invoices are more than 30 days overdue, she turns up at their building and politely waits for one of the finance department staff to come down to the reception area with her overdue cheque in hand. It never fails!

8. Maximize your bargaining power

Maximize your leverage. Try to establish how valuable the product you're selling is to your client. It may be a vital component in a manufacturing process, especially if it has been developed to the client's own specifications.

9. Monitor your risk portfolio

Keep abreast of news that may affect the creditworthiness of your key clients. Put their names on a low-cost monitoring service with a credit reference agency (Graydon's service is called CreditWatch). There is nothing worse than being the last to know when something has happened to one of your key customers. Don't fall into the trap of believing you know everything you need to know about your clients. A businessman I know was informed by a credit agency monitoring service that one of his clients had attracted a number of County Court Judgments over a few short weeks. As a result, he insisted on cash up front when the client's next order arrived in his in-tray. The client declined the offer on this occasion and put the phone down in an agitated mood. Two weeks later, that disgruntled client actually went bust owing several other unsecured trade creditors money! Thanks to his foresight in buying a monitoring service, my businessman friend avoided a potentially crippling bad debt. Losses from bad debts can really put a strain on a business's cash flow, and in the worst scenarios can even bring companies down! It's the old domino effect. You may not see all bad debts coming, but there are tools out there that can help minimize the chances of it happening, so why not use them like the credit professionals do?

10. Develop a 'friend'

Try to establish a personal rapport with one or two people in your client's accounts department. Get to know Gladys or Vera in the purchase ledger department, by engaging in some general conversation. What might seem like a time-wasting exercise asking Vera about her recent trip to the zoo could actually prove a very productive use of your time if she pulls out your invoice for payment when asked to do so a few moments later. In my experience, the personal touch never fails!

Summary

The message could not be clearer. If smaller businesses follow this advice, they will find that cash flow difficulties will ease. This course of action will be far better than doing nothing about slow payments, particularly from large organizations (apparently, half of small businesses continue to suffer slow payments in silence for fear of losing 'valuable accounts'), or doing the extreme opposite, ie closing the account. Two things are certain: large companies are not going to change their bullying payment habits overnight, and there will always be clients with genuine cash-flow difficulties that cannot pay up on time. Your organization may not yet be big enough to employ a professional credit manager, but taking the recommended steps above will make it look to the outside world like you do. This may well lead to you gaining not only respect from customers, but a healthier cash position for your business too!

For more information:

Graydon UK Limited – www.graydon.co.uk

Federation of Small Businesses – http://www.fsb.org.uk

The Better Payment Practice Group – http://www.payontime.co.uk

PAYMENTS COUNCIL

DRIVING CHANGE IN UK PAYMENTS

The Payments Council is the organisation that sets strategy for UK payments.

It works to ensure that UK payments systems and services meet the needs of users, payment service providers and the wider economy.

For more information about the Payments Council please contact us:

Telephone: 020 7711 6200
Email: press@ukpayments.org.uk

www.paymentscouncil.org.uk

Bill payment by direct credit – the importance of accurate referencing

Peter Finlayson, UK Payments Administration

Introduction

Following an extensive consultation process, the Payments Council published the National Payments Plan (NPP) in May 2008. The Plan identifies a number of UK payment service areas where there are gaps or potential scope for improvement. One such area relates to the reference information associated with direct credit automated payments.

In the UK, direct credit payments are made via Bacs Direct Credits, the Faster Payments Service (FPS) and CHAPS. They include consumer-initiated internet- and telephone-banking direct payments, as well as business-initiated direct payments. When a payment is made by direct credit, the payer must specify the bank sort code and account number of the payee, and it is normally also necessary to include reference information, defined as information which enables payers and payees to uniquely identify a transaction and link it to their internal records. This definition, therefore, includes explicit references such as an invoice number or customer account number entered into a reference field, but it also includes data such as the payer name. Missing or inaccurate reference information can be a serious problem for payees, who may have difficulty reconciling the payment, and it may also adversely affect payers and banks via knock-on effects.

The NPP consultation process revealed a widespread perception that there is scope for improvement in the area of direct credit payment reference information, leading to efficiency benefits for both users and payment service providers. Moreover, better referencing will support the migration to direct credits from less efficient payment methods such as cheques.

This is a complex, multi-faceted area that impacts many parts of the UK payments industry, where there appears to be a genuine appetite on the part of users and payment service providers for better solutions, and where the time was right to undertake a serious, focused review within the framework of the NPP. Accordingly, the Payments Council commissioned a research project in 2009 to understand and quantify the problems caused by missing or inaccurate reference information associated with direct credit payments, and to identify potential solutions. This chapter describes the results of that research and the best practice guidelines, which were the main recommendations arising out of the research. The research was restricted to UK direct credit payments: direct debits and standing orders. Card payments, payments via SWIFT, and cross-border direct credits were not covered.

Bill payments

Early in the research, it was established that bill payments accounted for the vast majority of reference-related problems.

These fell into two main areas. The first area comprised Consumer-to-Business (C2B) bill payments, such as consumers paying credit card bills by online or telephone banking. The second area comprised Business-to-Business (B2B) bill payments, such as business customers paying supplier invoices by Bacs, CHAPS or the Faster Payments Service.

Although direct credits are also used extensively for Business-to-Consumer (B2C) payments (eg salaries and benefit payments), and increasingly for Consumer-to-Consumer (C2C) payments (eg paying family and friends via online banking), reference information is less important for these types of payment.

C2B payments

C2B direct credit payments are characterized by a consumer paying a 'biller', such as a credit card company, utility or HMRC, via internet or telephone banking.[1] As shown in Figure 2.2.1 below, such 'push' payments only account for about four per cent of bill payments, but the absolute volume still amounts to about 225 million per annum, and can be expected to rise as payments by cheque are displaced. Direct debits and standing orders, 'pull' payments, are by far the most popular C2B payment methods, accounting for 62 per cent of the total.

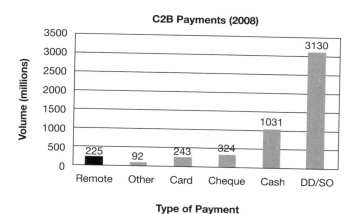

Figure 2.2.1 C2B payment volumes

Different types of billers use direct credits to very different extents, as shown in Figure 2.2.2. Payment of credit card bills is the most important category. By contrast, payment of bills for utilities, tax, councils and so on, account for a relatively small share of the total. Direct debit and standing order are much more popular payment methods for this type of payee.

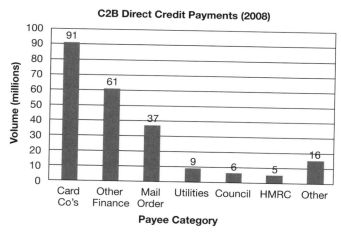

Figure 2.2.2 Direct credit payments by payee category

The experiences of best case and worst case billers differ by orders of magnitude. In the worst cases, the proportion of payments with reference-related problems can exceed 10 per cent and the unit cost of reconciliation can be of the order of £5. In the best cases, error rates can be less than one per cent and unit reconciliation costs of the order of 50p. The higher error rates relate to a relatively small proportion of direct credit payments, as the billers who receive the most payments by direct credit typically have the lowest error rates.

This wide variation suggests that there is scope for the billers who experience the worst problems to improve matters by adopting best practice from those who experience fewer problems (eg credit card companies and mail-order firms).

B2B Payments

B2B direct credits represent a much more complex and heterogeneous class of payment than C2B. In its simplest form, a single invoice is paid with a single payment, typically quoting the customer account number and/or invoice number as a reference. In many cases the payment covers several invoices and may cover more complex transactions, such as partly paid invoices or credit notes. In such cases, an associated Remittance Advice is more important than the payment itself in helping the payee determine what the payment is for, while the payment itself should help the payee determine who the payment is from, and must include a clear and unambiguous link to the associated Remittance Advice. The payment reference field normally acts as such a link, and may also help to identify the payer if it is in the form of a customer account number, although clearly it helps if the separate payer name field is also clear and unambiguous.

As shown in Figure 2.2.3, at 21 per cent of the total, direct credit payments account for a significantly higher proportion of B2B payments than is the case with C2B, and direct debits account for fewer, although they are becoming more important. The relative popularity of direct credits is a reflection of the control that they give to businesses making payments. Cheques are still the most popular means of payment, at 36 per cent of the total, but this proportion can be expected to drop as cheques are replaced by automated payment methods over the next decade, further increasing the importance of direct credits.

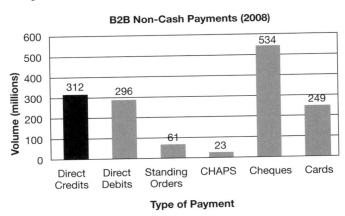

Figure 2.2.3 B2B payments by type

As with C2B payments, there is considerable variation in perceived payee problems, and therefore scope for best practice guidelines, but in addition the particular business context is important.

For many cases referencing is really not a major issue. This is certainly the case for very small businesses with few payments in or out. It is also the case for medium sized or large businesses with a fairly stable set of long-standing business partners, where, typically, ad hoc procedures evolve over time to meet the referencing needs of all parties. A special case of this model is where a tightly integrated trading group has been established (eg supermarkets and their suppliers). In such cases the payment is only one small part of a much larger 'trade documentation' process, and businesses use a variety of relatively sophisticated 'e-invoicing' tools and techniques with the ultimate aim of achieving 'Straight-Through-Processing'.

Trading models where referencing can be a serious problem, include conventional billers, such as utilities and telephone companies – the same organizations that account for the majority of C2B problems. Another group that experiences problems includes businesses such as insolvency practices or factoring operations, where there may be large numbers of relatively unknown counterparties with no prior business relationships, and in such circumstances missing, inaccurate or incomplete reference information can be a serious issue.

Not surprisingly, given such heterogeneity, the range of problems experienced by B2B payees is even more variable than in the C2B case.

Best practice guidelines

For C2B and B2B bill payments, the end-to-end process was analysed to understand how reference-related problems arise, how big they are, and how best practice can be applied.

Shown in Figure 2.2.4 is a generic representation of the end-to-end process.

Although the majority of referencing errors arise during payment by the payer, (stage 2), problems may arise at all stages and best practice needs to be applied end-to-end in the payment chain.

Four areas where there is scope to introduce best practice guidelines are considered below.

Billing best practice

Most billing best practice is largely common sense: for example, using simple customer references that are prominently displayed on the bill, designing the bill so that payment options are explained simply, clearly and unambiguously, and explaining that for direct credit payments the correct reference must be entered accurately.

On most bills, from utility companies for example, the actual instructions for paying by direct credit are reasonably straightforward, but the reference to be used is often found overleaf, sometimes only on the bank giro credit, and sometimes not prominently displayed or labelled. The instructions themselves may be hidden within a large range of payment options. And the reference itself may be complex, with special characters or gaps.

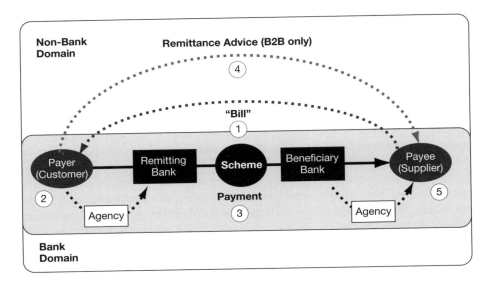

Figure 2.2.4 Generic end-to-end payment process

Some B2B invoices are fairly straightforward and simply instruct payment to be made to a specified bank account. However, although the invoice number is usually displayed prominently at the top of the invoice, the instructions often do not make it clear that the invoice number should be used as a reference, or what other information should be used if this is not the case. The range of invoices is immense and many do not indicate which bank details are to be used, never mind references.

Payment best practice

Most retail online banking systems feature drop-down lists of common billers, or equivalent search facilities, with their collection account details. Once a direct credit payment has been set up, with an appropriate reference, it is then stored as a template to be used for subsequent payments. But there is considerable variation across banks with respect to terminology, conventions, layout, and the degree of prompting to enter a meaningful reference. This is an area where adoption of consistent best practice could result in an improved consumer experience.

The process of updating drop-down menus, templates, and formats is fairly ad hoc and reliant on billers remembering to update all banks. There is a case for considering a more coordinated, central function here.

Payment transmission best practice

An important consideration is the extent to which reference information is passed end-to-end from remitting bank, to beneficiary bank, through agency banks, to the ultimate payee. For C2B and B2B payments, end-to-end delivery to the business payee always occurs, and the reference information is reliably displayed on the payee's statement, or at least made available online. However this does not always happen for B2C payments. Best practice guidelines could promote greater end-to-end transmission of reference information for payments to personal customers.

Reconciliation best practice

No matter how reliable the other parts of the end-to-end payments process, there will always be payments with missing or inaccurate reference information that need to be reconciled. In addition to the payment reference itself, payees may use any or all of the following types of information to reconcile payments:

■ Payer name. This is very important, not only when a payment reference is missing or inaccurate, but also when the payment detail may be held in a Remittance Advice that may arrive several days after the payment itself. In such circumstances, the payee needs to know who the payment is from so that it can be posted immediately, without necessarily knowing what the payment is for. The payer name normally defaults to the short account name (truncated to 18 characters), which is not always very meaningful to the payee.
■ Payment amount. This can also be very helpful for reconciling payments.
■ Remitting bank details. Many businesses use the remitting bank sort code and account number to identify who a payment is from. This information is always present in Bacs payments and is used routinely to identify payments from customers who have paid before. It may also be used to identify first-time payments if the biller captures a customer's remitting bank details as a contractual condition of trading. The solution is not 100 per cent reliable – a payer may make a payment from a different account, or a third party may pay on their behalf – but in practice it seems to work well.
■ Inputs from Credit Management and Collections. Best practice is for all departments involved with incoming payments and dealing with customers to work closely together, supported by integrated systems. For example, if a customer is chased for a late payment by a service centre and it transpires that because of referencing problems the payment has been allocated to a suspense account, then the accounts receivable department needs to be informed, an appropriate memo added to the customer records, and ideally, the customer should be educated so that the same problem does not recur. All too often, this does not happen. As a more general point, regular, prompt and coordinated corporate communication with customers tends to be associated with low referencing error rates.

Several larger businesses make use of automated reconciliation systems that use some or all of these types of information. The most sophisticated systems 'learn' with experience. Such systems may be developed in-house or may be supplied by vendors.

Bank responsiveness to payee reconciliation requests is another area where there may be scope for improvement. Payee experience tends to be dependent on the

relationship with a particular bank, or with a particular branch or on which individual within the bank happens to deal with the query.

Next steps

In summary, the research has demonstrated that missing or inaccurate reference
information is indeed a significant issue for some bill payments by direct credit and
indicated that there may be considerable scope for improvement simply by adopting fairly straightforward best practice guidelines.

The Payments Council has agreed to take the lead in developing and disseminat-
ing the guidelines in a coordinated fashion. As with the original research, the work
will be undertaken in close collaboration with key stakeholders. The Payments
Council will also investigate other areas where there may be potential to improve
the use of referencing information, such as greater coordination in updating biller
reference formats on internet banking sites.

Note

1   For the purposes of the research, telephone banking is regarded as equivalent
to online banking, in the sense that the telephone operator is assumed to use
the same online banking system. Banks confirmed that, in general, this was the
case. In 2008, about two-thirds of remote payments were via online banking
(21.5 million and rising), and about one-third via telephone banking (12.3
million and falling).

Revenue Relationships Results

They're what matter most to you. Us too.

Our expertise in collections and recovery is born out of a global heritage in customer relationship management. No one understands better than we do what makes customers tick, how to keep them close, or how to influence their behaviour in your favour.

So, when it comes to collections and recoveries, trust Transcom to deliver the results you need. **Strong revenues. Profitable relationships.**

Trust Transcom

- Services across the debt lifecycle - from early collections to legal recovery
- Serving a global client base from 79 locations in 25 countries including the UK
- Segmented collection strategies supported by analytics

Talk to Transcom and find out how we can help you manage what matters.

The search for solid ground – outsourcing to stabilize your debt management performance

Mike Purvis, Transcom Worldwide (UK)

Introduction

Throughout the recession the number of UK consumers and businesses falling into catastrophic debt (the point at which their indebtedness exceeds their ability to pay) has grown relentlessly. And, though technical recovery may be on its way, it's likely to be a long time yet before confidence returns or finances ease. Scarcely a company in the country hasn't seen its cash flow damaged and its list of debtors rise. But, almost as worrying as the rise in debt is the fall in predictability. Established patterns of payment and default are shifting, placing pressure on credit management staff and systems that must struggle to deal with them; and upon businesses unused to living with the financial uncertainty those shifting patterns bring.

To date most credit management departments have looked to outsourcing as a tactical measure to address short-term challenges or to reduce their losses on hard-core debt. In this chapter, Transcom – one of the world's largest outsourced credit management and debt collection providers – invites you to consider whether a more far-reaching approach to outsourcing can help regain the stability lost in recent months and provide the solid ground upon which a new approach to customers and debt can be built.

The recent recession has given rise to three factors that have thrown credit management departments into disarray. First and most obviously, the sheer number of debtors – and levels of debt they incur – has increased. Because this has, for most companies, been accompanied by a fall in sales volume, the pressure on cash flow has been intense. It has led board directors to apply significant pressure on their credit management departments to recover debt quickly, and to take aggressive measures if necessary.

Second, even 'good' payers have become 'slow' payers. Customers who would typically pay on the nose when the invoice became due are extending their payment terms – from 30 days to 60, or from 60 to 90. This is compounded by the fact that many of the traditional instruments, such as invoice factoring, that have allowed companies to ease their way through payment intervals are simply not available or, like most sources of credit, have become too expensive to access.

Finally, the nature of debtors has changed. It isn't just that more customers are defaulting on their payments, but that – all too often – the default has been unexpected and unpredictable. Many of those now in payment arrears have previously been 'good' customers, but they now find themselves to be 'reluctant debtors' forced by circumstances they can't control into situations they can't remedy. With this group an aggressive debt collection approach will be expensive and rarely deliver results. After all, the problem isn't that they 'won't' pay; it is, quite simply, that they 'can't'.

The reluctant debtor – two definitions:

■ Careful spenders on tight budgets whose ability to live within their means is challenged either by unprecedented rises in the cost of living or sudden loss of income through redundancy, pay cuts or short working.
■ Sophisticated spenders who manage debt responsibly, meeting payments and moving debt around to secure the best lending deals. But, with property prices depressed and sources of consumer credit all but dried up, they've lost their room to manoeuvre.

And the number of individuals likely to fall into the reluctant debtor category is extremely high, simply because of the way the British public's approach to debt has changed over the past 10 to 15 years. When the United Kingdom last went into recession in the early 1990s, levels of consumer debt in Britain were significantly lower than they were when we entered the current one, when, at around £1.4 trillion, they were the highest in Europe and almost level with GDP. More and more individuals now see indebtedness as a natural state that they manage diligently. It does, however, place them on a knife-edge, making them highly vulnerable to financial crisis when the economy turns sour.

A unique bind

Three factors leave credit management departments in a unique and torturous bind. First, the pure volume of default means they have more debt to manage than people to manage it. We've come across companies struggling to manage increases in debtor numbers of anywhere between 20 per cent and 100 per cent. Unsurprisingly, their pleas to recruit additional staff to deal with that increase fall on deaf ears within their cash-strapped organizations.

Second, the changing debtor profile means that their tried and tested approaches simply no longer work; yet they have limited ability to change them. At the very moment when they need to introduce more flexible approaches to debt collection – instalment plans or 'payment holidays' for reluctant debtors, for example – they're discovering that the technology systems they depend upon simply can't support them. Its surprising how many credit management departments still rely on inflexible billing systems rather than dedicated credit management support infra-structures – we estimate around seven in ten. And, once again, this probably isn't the best time in the world to be asking the board for technology investment!

Finally, the challenges presented by inflexible systems are compounded by inappropriate skills. In strong economies credit management is a largely 'administrative' task. Most late payments are the result of oversight or accident rather than an inability to pay or determination not to. The small minority of 'genuine' debt is managed through standard processes that escalate – typically after a 90-day period – to a legal process, usually involving the company's in-house or external counsel. Credit management teams have been built accordingly, with a base team of 'progress chasers' supplemented by a small number of debt managers whose predominant expertise is legal. Few coalface staff have the relationship-manage-ment skills needed to adopt varied approaches according to the debtor profile; to take a sensitive, conciliatory approach with reluctant debtors, while progressing determinedly with hard core 'won't pay' individuals.

All of this means that most organizations find themselves on shifting sands as far as debt is concerned. Their ability to predict, manage and recover it is severely compromised, while their options to recruit new skills or develop new approaches are financially constrained. In this climate, outsourcing – which allows people, processes and technologies to be accessed by means of variable cost rather than capital investment – must seem like an attractive option.

Far-sighted organizations are looking to external partners who, in the first instance, can help them overcome their short-term staffing requirements, but who can also address their entire debt management life cycle – from credit risk assess-ment of new customers, through invoicing, dispute handling, collections and enforcement. They are looking to these organizations to bring stability to their finances and to fast-track the development of sophisticated new approaches that will meet their needs through recession, recovery and beyond.

Those new approaches will, for the most part, be focused around three guiding principles:

■ the use of advanced customer management approaches to manage reluctant debtors;
■ the adoption of analytics-based techniques and technologies to implement a risk-based approach to debt management;
■ the use of flexible payment models to keep cash coming in and to prevent expensive escalation.

Let's look at each in turn.

Managing customers or pursuing debt

With the United Kingdom's currently unprecedented levels of consumer indebtedness, it's a sad fact of life that debt is no longer an aberration, but an integral part of the typical customer experience. Yet most organizations treat 'customer relationship management' and 'credit management' as two completely different disciplines, housed within departmental silos. Skilled outsourcers bring them together, using finely tuned customer management skills to manage reluctant debtors; to probe, empathize and negotiate. And to implement flexible payment plans that deliver results for both parties.

For example, if a reluctant debtor simply can't afford the monthly minimum repayment of £100 on their loan, it probably makes sense to accept a lower payment, providing they commit to an agreed repayment schedule. This at least keeps some funds coming in and the two parties still talking. After all, what's the alternative? If an impasse is reached and no payment is made the debt will escalate into a post-90-day legal process that's costly, delivers poor results and is likely to destroy the customer relationship along the way. Remember, when the immediate crisis is over, these customers are likely to return to their usual good financial health – becoming once again the valuable customers you've known them to be. The only way to maintain your share of their future prosperity is by taking an approach that favours conciliation and arbitration, delivered by an operation that's targeted on retention and rehabilitation as well as debt recovery.

Analysing the risk

If we accept that future success depends upon managing customers rather than debt, we can view debt not as an isolated incident, but as a natural part of the life-cycle that begins the minute the customer comes onboard; and we can manage the risk accordingly.

An analysis of historical customer data will reveal the commonly shared characteristics of those who have defaulted on payment to your organization. This, coupled with established geo-demographic profiling standards, makes it possible to forecast other customers' likelihood to default – both those you have already and those you hope to bring onboard. An appropriate risk score can then be applied that will govern the way that customer is managed. For example, a credit card company will take a cautious approach when extending credit limits for a customer with a high-risk score. By the same token, a mobile phone operator might choose not to proactively offer a contract option to a high-risk customer on a 'pay as you go' deal.

Analytics will also help predict which collections approach is most likely to meet with success. For example, we've been able to identify particular demographic segments – call them 'experienced' or 'wily' debtors, if you like – who will allow debt to escalate but pay immediately and in full when a legal process is threatened or undertaken. The best policy in these cases then – potentially disastrous in others, as we've discussed – will be to move to litigation quickly.

Quite simply, a risk-based approach allows companies to make a direct correlation between the level and type of risk posed by an individual customer and the way they are treated – both before they get into debt (how much credit do you extend) and after (what recovery approach do you take).

For example, on behalf of an internet service provider we work for, we use risk scores to determine our response when a client exceeds their credit limit or their daily usage increases uncharacteristically. A low-risk customer is sent a gentle customer care message in the first instance and the escalation process that follows is measured and 'soft touch'. A high-risk customer will receive an immediate phone call, followed by a much more assertive process.

Building flexibility

If analytics provides the insight needed to fuel a segmented, risk-based approach towards customers and their debts, it rests with technology to provide the engine. While companies continue to manage their credit operations via inflexible billing systems their progress will be hampered. For example, we've worked with companies whose internal systems, programmed to issue an invoice and recognize its payment in full – simply can't accommodate partial payments, deferrals or payment by instalment. They found themselves facing a simple choice, either take on a time-consuming and laborious manual process to reconcile the payments, or turn their back on flexible payment options. Both choices would have cost money. If a debtor was able to pay, say 75 per cent of the bill, they'd likely have felt inclined to accept and call it quits. But, if they'd been able to be flexible, they might have been able to recover 85 per cent or 90 per cent of the debt, through several payments made over a longer time period.

Fortunately, by outsourcing to us, they managed to avoid both of these expensive scenarios.

Buy 'results'

Which brings us to a final point about outsourcing. Cost. We've established that the landscape of debt in Britain has changed dramatically in the last 15 years. The evolution of credit management departments – by and large – has not kept pace. The pressure is now on to develop the kind of sophisticated approaches, supported by advanced credit management systems and analytics, quickly. The fastest way to do so is by working with a specialist partner, leveraging their skills, insights and processes.

New contracting models which share risk and reward by linking vendor remuneration to success mean you're able to buy 'results' rather than 'activity'. In short, they allow you to create a direct link between the price you pay and three key success measures:

- the percentage of debt recovered;
- the percentage of debt recovered without recourse to expensive legal action;
- a falling incidence of debt achieved through a risk-based approach to the pre-debt customer relationship.

Some of the most innovative outsourcing deals go further still by removing fixed asset burdens and even providing a much-needed cash injection. There is now an established trend towards leveraged outsourcing deals, in which the outsourced service provider takes over not just credit management activities currently undertaken in-house, but the staff responsible for them, the premises in which they're housed and the infrastructure on which they depend. The first benefit comes in terms of the fair market value paid for the fixed assets. The second in the alleviation of long-term asset management cost. The third, from the outsourcer's commitment not just to 'take over' but 'transform' the adopted operation, delivering ongoing operating cost reduction and performance improvement on an agreed glide path.

For organizations that have previously thought of outsourcing as a 'short-term fix' this will be revolutionary thinking indeed. But, for those eager to exchange instability for solid ground, it presents a realistic and achievable way forward.

PALADIN
COMMERCIAL CREDIT MANAGEMENT

35 Chalk Hill, Oxhey, Watford, WD19 4BL
Phone: 01923 800 397
Fax: 01923 237 911
General Enquiries: sales@paladincommercial.co.uk

At **Paladin Commercial Credit Management** we specialise in assisting a wide range of businesses in improving their cash flow. Experts in debt recovery, sales ledger management and litigation, the team at Paladin works with our client partners to simplify their credit management challenges and improve the value of its receivables.

We pride ourselves in our service proposition to our business partners developing long term relationships which are built upon effective communication and a common goal. Our business culture is open and transparent and our commercial fee structure ensures that you do not pay for unrecovered debts. Since inception in 1995 Paladin has collected over £120mm worth of its customers overdue receivables and concluded over 40,000 accounts nurturing an impressive portfolio of business clients which range from small to medium enterprises through to International Corporations.

In recent times our clients' needs have evolved resulting in Paladin's expansion of its business services. In addition to credit management and debt collections we now operate in the Debt Purchase and Invoice Discount markets where our clients prefer to sell their receivables thereby removing them from their balance sheet. Having secured private investor funding, Paladin is actively developing our own portfolio of acquired receivables.

www.paladincommercial.co.uk

The collections industry

George Miles,
Paladin Commercial Credit Management

Introduction

At Paladin Commercial Credit Management we specialize in assisting a wide range of businesses to improve their cash flow. Experts in debt recovery, sales ledger management and litigation, the team at Paladin works with client partners to simplify their credit management challenges and improve the value of its receivables.

Paladin prides itself in its service proposition to business partners, developing long-term relationships that are built upon effective communication and a common goal. Its business culture is open and transparent and its commercial fee structure ensures that clients do not pay for unrecovered debts.

Since its inception in 1995 Paladin has collected over £120 million worth of its customers' overdue receivables and concluded over 40,000 accounts, nurturing an impressive portfolio of business clients that range from small to medium enterprises through to international corporations.

In recent times clients' needs have evolved, resulting in expansion of Paladin's business services. In addition to credit management and debt collections it now operates in the debt purchase and invoice discount markets, where clients may prefer to sell their receivables in order to remove them from their balance sheets. Having secured private investor funding, Paladin is actively developing its own portfolio of acquired receivables.

The collections industry

In many ways, therefore, Paladin reflects the journey that the collections industry as a whole has undertaken over the past decade, facing up to the requirements of its customers, the creditors, by becoming ever more complex and diverse.

In one of its recent guides to the collections industry, the Credit Services Agency (CSA) shows how the industry has evolved and now services debts for clients across a huge range of sectors, including banks, building societies, credit card companies, telephone companies and the government and its various agencies such as HM Revenue & Customs, the Driver and Vehicle Licensing Agency and the Department for Work and Pensions.

The process debt collection agencies follow is similar to those employed by the creditor's own teams. Initial contact is usually by letter from the agent, giving the debtor the opportunity to settle the outstanding balance. If the initial contact is ignored, further correspondence may be sent, and the risk of legal action may be explained.

Why debt collection agencies are used?

The benefits for creditors in using an external expert revolves around the fact that members of the CSA are experts in what it takes to collect a debt in an efficient, responsible and ethical fashion. Debt collectors have only one focus: collections. So they are expert at it. Their employees are experts at it, and have experience and exposure to thousands of debtors and debt scenarios every week.

It is a fact of life that some consumers simply do not take a debt seriously until it is passed into the hands of a third party. At that point, the debt attains a new level of 'seriousness', and on many occasions the very first contact by an agency is sufficient for a debt to be settled.

The shape of the industry

There are an estimated 20,000 people in either a full- or part-time capacity employed by members of the CSA. Dramatic changes in technology have meant big changes in the way the credit industry and, therefore, the prevention and recovery of debt operate. Major databases supply fast and reliable credit information on companies and individuals.

Much of the collection process is by post and increasingly by email, SMS and telephone messaging. But there comes a point when human intervention is required.

Debt sale and purchase

Debt sale is the selling on of a debt by a business to a third-party debt buyer, for collection, at an appropriate price. The price is determined by the quality of the debt, and may range from a few pence in the pound for so-called 'gone away' or warehoused portfolios, up to 80 or more pence for the better quality debts with a commensurately better chance of recovery.

Debt has been sold in the United Kingdom for around 15 years and the annual market is estimated to be worth approximately £7 billion. Buyers and sellers undertake rigorous due diligence before any sale is made or any potential purchaser is added to the panel. Creditors have no more wish to put their reputations at risk after a sale than in a traditional commission-based scenario and so they look for responsible debt buyers.

It is a market where Paladin has considerable experience.

Should your business wish to monetize the value tied up in its bad debt accounts or simply accelerate the cash flow from its delinquent portfolio, industry experts such as Paladin are active in the debt purchase market and would be keen to conduct a prompt portfolio valuation. Those with secured private funding, such as Paladin, can be flexible and move quickly in the agreement and execution of sale and purchase contracts allowing a client business to free significant capital tied up in its distressed receivables.

The timetable for evaluating, pricing and purchasing trade debt portfolios can be quite elongated as portfolio trades can become complex due to funding restrictions and limitations. As the economic environment has become more demanding, Paladin clients have benefited from its ability to be flexible and move quickly.

The principal advantage for the creditor is clearly that debt sale provides a business with the certainty of a guaranteed cash injection, supporting P&L and balance sheet needs. This can be critical to both financial controller and company alike. Debts that might otherwise have to be written off will achieve some value.

But it is important to note that there are more 'added-value' advantages, including freeing up credit managers and their teams to focus on more value-efficient activities. Rather than chasing apparent lost causes, they can devote time to improving forward cash flow and early collections. Easing the administrative burden also helps to ease costs.

Invoice discounting

If your business operates an invoice credit policy for its customers or offers interest-free credit or a sales aid credit agreement, there may be circumstances where you would benefit from selling these trade receivables to improve cash flow. Alternatively, the costs associated with administering credit control and collections, together with the work involved in chasing overdue accounts, may lead you to consider a regular sale of outstanding receivables.

At Paladin, we have acquired client partners' outstanding invoices and sales aid credit agreements, assisting their business models, allowing them to increase sales in a challenging market. We have also entered into repeat flow agreements providing clients with a monthly or quarterly drawdown against receivables.

The collectors

The collection professional on the telephone is the mainstay of any collections agency or debt purchaser, with trained negotiators making the first contact with the debtor.

Personal characteristics required by a collector, which the CSA highlights and which Paladin certainly look for are:

- excellent communication skills in both speech and writing;
- an enquiring mind;
- tact and diplomacy in dealing with people;
- the ability to be understanding, yet assertive;
- a good judge of character;
- negotiating skills;
- keyboard and computer skills.

Dialogue

CSA work on a simple understanding, which is matched throughout the industry: that the key to successful debt recovery is to develop a positive dialogue with the debtor to discuss and decide on the right pathway that will get them to pay.

Collectors try to distinguish between those that cannot pay, and those that will not pay. It is not an easy task, but one of which Paladin has considerable experience and so is able to understand the motivations of debtors and to deal with them responsibly and appropriately. In this way both customers and debtors are treated fairly and responsibly and, at the same time, the best results are achieved. It is essential that debtors do not stick their heads in the sand. Ignoring contact will create more problems than it solves.

Petition

Debt collection is an important job, one that can be difficult and is often misunderstood by government and the national media.

As a result, the major trade publication *Credit Collections & Risk* has placed a petition before the government asking that it should back the industry in its efforts to collect debts fairly and ethically and that it should encourage consumers to appreciate that they have a moral duty to pay what they owe.

The petition has been placed on the prime minister's website: www.number10. gov.uk. It contends that the collections and enforcement industry is, in terms of fairness and the efforts made to treat customers professionally and ethically, one of the leading sectors of the UK economy. It asks that the government should show public support for the industry and encourage consumers to understand their moral duty to pay what they owe, to agreed terms or as quickly as they reasonably can.

The petition reads:

We the undersigned petition the Prime Minister to make a public statement of support for the Collections and Enforcement industry, acknowledging that it is made up of some of the most professional and ethical companies in the whole of UK economy.

Although, in any industry, it is right to highlight and root out bad practice, we believe the national media coverage of the Collections and Enforcement industry is routinely unfair and not representative.

We call on the Government to make a statement to promote the good work done by the Collections and Enforcement industry and to encourage consumers and the national media to consider that people have a moral duty to repay what they owe, where they reasonably can, and that the Collections and Enforcement industry has the right and the responsibility to try to collect in a responsible fashion, which it does in the overwhelming majority of cases.

If consumers do not pay then – just like good drivers having to pay for bad drivers through higher insurance premiums – everyone will suffer in higher interest rates and charges.

At the time of writing, the petition had nearly 400 signatories.

This is a huge issue for the country as the economy struggles to emerge from recession. Collectors work hard to support those debtors who have genuine difficulties in paying and who will work with them, but all debtors should also understand that they have a moral duty to pay back what they owe. This is no victimless crime; if they do not pay back what they owe, then just like insurance premiums having to go up for bad drivers, everyone has to pay through higher interest rates or charges.

Collectability Index

Against this background, the collections industry is working hard to provide an outstanding service for is clients.

The CSA's recent Collectability Index found that that there has recently been a stabilization of consumers' ability or willingness to repay their debts.

The principal themes to emerge from the Index in the first two quarters of 2009 – researched by the CSA and The Debt Buyers & Sellers Group – is that both the index of instalments and the index of settlements have stabilized in the first two quarters of 2009, following a continuous decline in 2008. This indicates that we are in a bottoming-out period of consumers' ability to pay. An average of 33 per cent of consumers were able or willing to fully settle their debts in the first two quarters in 2008 compared with an average of only 25 per cent for the same period of 2009. This represents a decline of 24 per cent between the two periods.

However, the report – which aims to be a quarterly barometer to determine a debtor's ability to pay, measured by the volumes and values reported – emphasizes that these are early indicators only and that no firm conclusion can be reached until quarters three and four of 2009 and, going forward, perhaps even the quarter one 2010 outcomes are known.

In particular, given the worsening employment figures that the government recently reported, it will be some time before the industry can genuinely know whether the bottom has already been reached in terms of collectability performance.

Conclusion

However, the economy continues to move and, regardless of how collectability rates respond, there will still be a real need for creditors to access the best quality skills to collect debts and keep cash flowing into the business.

At Paladin, our collection experience can be used by any type of business which grants credit to its customers. Whether you are experiencing difficulty in being paid or have insufficient resources to chase your debtors, Paladin can help as experts in debt collection.

The importance of business partners' relationships with their customers is recognized and a strict code of conduct and professionalism is applied, which does not compromise. Expertise, technology and an assertive culture consistently achieve high-quality results, thereby maximizing clients' cash flow.

a better way forward

Lowell Group has developed a way of working which sets us apart.

We go the extra mile to treat people fairly, openly and honestly, whether they are our clients in the boardroom or the debtor on the end of a phone.

Our people are part of a culture of trust, involvement and innovation and this allows us to maximise their input and help them to realise their potential. Our clients are confident in us as we put them at the heart of everything we do.

In terms of systems, no company in our sector gives a higher priority to technology than Lowell Group. This ensures we gain optimum efficiency, integration and productivity.

Lowell Group has risen to become a significant force within our market. We believe this is because we do things better.

Our commitment to staying at the forefront of our industry directly benefits our clients and we are committed to maintaining our position as leaders in our market delivering better results.

**get to know Lowell Group better
call us on 0845 279 7123**

Lowell. a better way forward
GROUP

An introduction to debt sale and purchase

Joyce Newman, Lowell Group

Historically, lenders tended to carry out debt collection activities in-house until they reached a certain level of delinquency at which point they would be outsourced to a debt collection agency on a commission basis.

The concept of selling debt was developed in the United States in the late 1980s and spread to the United Kingdom around five years later when US credit card companies, already experienced in debt sale, started entering the UK market. Since then debt sale has grown rapidly, helped considerably by the growth of the UK consumer finance market

Over the last 15 years, until the recent credit crunch, the UK consumer finance market experienced a compound annual growth rate of around 10 per cent. Economic factors including strong growth in GDP, low interest rates, high levels of employment and continuously rising house prices had created market conditions where consumers were confident in taking on personal debt and lenders were very happy to lend.

In December 1993 total UK personal debt (secured and unsecured) stood at £400 billion. By August 2009 the total had more than trebled to £1,457 billion.

In simple terms, debt sale involves lenders selling on portfolios of consumer debt – typically non-performing ones – to specialist debt buyers. The buyers themselves are collections specialists who are also skilled in assessing the value of portfolios. Having bought the debts, they are entitled to keep all the monies they collect rather than being paid on a commission basis by the lender.

The benefits of debt sale

There are several reasons why lenders would want to sell debt portfolios. One of the main ones is that it crystallizes the value of the debt – providing a business with a guaranteed income now versus an uncertain income spread over several years ahead against which the costs of collection would need to be offset.

In addition, the cost of administering the debts disappears and it frees up credit managers and their teams to focus on more productive activities, such as working towards improving forward cash flow and early collections.

More recently, two regulatory factors have boosted the appeal of debt sale. First, the introduction of International Accounting Standard 39, which requires expected recoveries to be discounted at a rate that is often over 10 per cent and can therefore create significant impairments to asset values.

Secondly, debt sale has benefited from the introduction of BASEL II regulations, which has resulted in lenders aiming to improve capital ratios by reducing 'at risk' loan balances.

Selling debt has therefore become an important profit and loss, balance sheet and risk management tool for many companies.

Market development

As a result the market has evolved considerably over the last 15 years. Now almost all the United Kingdom's major personal credit providers sell portfolios of debt. Most are financial services companies – banks, building societies, credit card and loan companies – but regular sellers also include retailers, mail-order businesses and, more recently, mobile phone and other communication companies.

Not only has the range of sellers expanded but also the types of debt portfolios being sold. In the early years most portfolios were of low quality, only put up for sale at or near the stage of being written off completely, which meant typically they would have:

■ been delinquent for at least two years;
■ been placed with three or more external collection agencies;
■ a high proportion of 'trace' accounts – without current address/contact details;
■ already been subject to some form of legal recovery attempt.

One of the major concerns sellers had about selling debt was (and still is) the 'reputational risk'. They thought they might be seen as washing their hands of the debt and potentially selling it to a company that might not treat account holders properly or fairly.

However, as sellers have gained experience with the purchasers and confidence in the process and its benefits, they have been willing to sell portfolios earlier in the recovery cycle, where the prospect of collection, and therefore the value, is higher. Today, many organizations will consider selling debts within six months of delinquency without ever placing them with a debt collections agent. In fact, some organizations are now opting to sell non-delinquent 'performing debt'. The sophistication of modern scoring techniques means they are able to identify accounts that potentially could underperform or turn delinquent before they actually do!

Debt purchasers have played a key role in growing the market by developing more accurate pricing models, more effective collections strategies and better control systems for ensuring fair and ethical treatment of their customers and compliance with ever-increasing regulation of the industry.

Over the years the relationship between buyers and sellers has become far more transparent, which has benefited both sides. There is far more sharing of information, including collections performance data, which ultimately means better customer management.

The sale process

Debt sale starts with the seller informing prospective buyers of the bidding process, type of contract and proposed contract terms. The bidding process will usually involve buyers submitting an initial bid from which shortlisted candidates will be given access to more detailed information on the portfolio and invited to submit a final bid. Contracts terms will usually be pre-agreed before final bids are invited.

The portfolio data given to prospective buyers for pricing and due diligence typically includes personal data – name, address, telephone number, date of birth, home ownership – plus data on the debt – account open date and default dates, historic payment data and balance for sale.

The main types of contract are spot, forward flow and right to collect. Spot is a one-off sale of a portfolio, whereas forward flow is where the seller agrees to sell the purchaser a volume of debt every month for a given period, usually 3 to 12 months. Right to collect is different in that the seller does not allow full legal assignment of the debt to the purchaser – only the right to collect the debt for a pre-agreed period, typically between 5 and 10 years.

Contract terms will cover post-sale arrangements for handing over the portfolio, dealing with customer queries and complaints, rights of recourse (if, for example, a debtor is deceased, in prison or bankrupt), rights for onward sale and rights to outsource collection. Rights for onward sale and rights to outsource will typically be restricted and not allowed without prior agreement from the seller.

Portfolio acquisition

Determining an accurate price for a portfolio is singularly the largest exposure for a debt purchaser and also the largest reason why a portfolio may be awarded to one purchaser over another. It is therefore no surprise that this is the area in which understanding the data available and the use of this data is of most importance.

Buyers use sophisticated models to analyse and segment the account data they receive and most will also invest in appending datasets from third parties such as credit bureaux, although they are prevented at this stage from accessing consumer credit files.

Given that many portfolios sold contain a significant percentage of accounts where there has been no contact from the debtor for a year or more, some purchasers will go to the extent of performing a sample tracing exercise to validate contact details and more accurately assess the likelihood of effecting collection.

Debtor tracing – the ability to find account holders – is fundamental to collecting effectively since all portfolios, even younger, fresher ones, will contain accounts for which data may not be up to date. Many purchasers still rely on manual-based tracing methods; purchasers with an automated tracing system have a distinct competitive advantage.

Armed with this intelligence, management are in a better position to make more informed pricing decisions, taking into account their own previous experience of similar portfolios and other factors such as prevailing market prices.

Optimizing collections

Once a deal has been concluded, the purchaser will spend a good amount of time prior to loading accounts on to the system cleaning, pre-analysing and scoring the data so that different collections strategies can be set for different categories of account. The process is likely to involve a post address finder (PAF) validating the address, appending new telephone numbers using data sets such as BT Operator Services Information System (OSIS) and screening for people who are deceased, bankrupt or have an Individual Voluntary Agreement in place. Significantly, at this stage the debt buyer is allowed to have access to the account holders' full credit file from the credit reference bureaux, which is very important for establishing propensity to pay. It is essential that the most vulnerable debtors – those who can't pay – are accurately identified so that an appropriate strategy to help them can be applied.

Most collection strategies involve each account moving through a carefully structured, relatively automated telephone and letter communication regime designed in the first instance to re-engage with the customer and help them to consider solutions to their outstanding debt problems, then to start and maintain repayments. Throughout the process intelligent use of data plays a vital role in optimizing collections efficiency. For example, by tracking payment patterns and monitoring customer quality characteristics it is possible to build propensity to default and propensity to settle early models.

Regulation and treating customers fairly

Debt purchasers must treat their customers fairly and are required to comply with a variety of standards of conduct and regulations, most notably the Consumer

Credit Act 1974/2006, the Office of Fair Trading (OFT) Debt Collection Guidance and the Data Protection Act 1998.

The Consumer Credit Act requires debt purchasers to apply for and hold a consumer credit licence. It is issued by the OFT and has to be renewed every five years. To be considered fit to hold a licence, debt purchasing companies must follow the OFT's 'debt collection guidance'. This guidance is based on the Debt Buyers & Sellers Group's own voluntary code of conduct. The OFT has the authority to visit and audit companies at any time. If it discovers breaches of the guidance, it can impose 'requirements' on the company to change its procedures. Serious breaches could lead to a company having its licence revoked.

The Data Protection Act governs how personal data is used and processed and, as such, is particularly pertinent to debt buyers. To put things into perspective, Lowell Group, the United Kingdom's leading debt purchasing company, has more than five million customers, 400 staff and deals with over 1.2 million letters and 150,000 telephone calls, in and out, every month.

As a market leader Lowell is spending £1 in every £20 of its overhead costs on compliance and maintains a 17-strong in-house compliance team. In addition, the company places great emphasis on staff training, including putting every new collector through a three-months training academy programme.

Both the consumer lending and debt collection industries have come under the media spotlight in recent months, which in turn has attracted the attention of regulators. Legislation in the debt industry is certain to increase, putting additional pressure on both buyers and sellers to ensure compliance.

The future

Short term, the credit crunch has had a negative effect in a number of respects. It has put consumers under pressure, causing debt recovery rates to fall. It has slowed down the growth rate in consumer credit and prompted lenders to become more circumspect in their lending decisions, which will ultimately impact on debt portfolios made available for sale. At the same time debt buyers are finding it more difficult to raise the finance to fund portfolio purchases. As a result, after 15 years of rising prices sellers are now seeing the prices paid for their portfolios falling. To counteract this, sellers have been adopting different sales strategies, including segmenting portfolios before sale to drive up returns and offering portfolios on a hybrid sale/contingency basis.

Long term, the prospects for debt sale/purchase remain good. As the UK market matures, buyers and sellers are learning to work more closely together, forming strategic partnerships where the risks and rewards are shared.

The growth and development of the debt purchase sector in the UK has seen individual organizations develop specialist areas of expertise, which is opening up the possibility of a secondary sale market – the sale of portfolios from one debt purchaser to another. Until now this has been constrained because of original vendors' concerns over reputational risk, but attitudes are changing.

Meanwhile the public sector and utilities sector are potential new markets for debt sale. The public sector has used DCAs for several years and legislation is now starting to be passed that will allow government agencies to start selling debt – possibilities include student loans, child support and court fines.

Part 3

Innovation and success in managing credit

Proactive credit management is key for successful customer relationships and business continuity

Maarten de Wild,
OnGuard Credit Management Software

The current economic climate has increased focus on working capital. A lot of companies are facing liquidity problems. Loans are hard to get or very expensive. Because invoices are being paid later and later and there is a greater risk of bankruptcy of major customers, credit management must be given top priority by Boards and Executive Management. Best of breed software can take you to a next level of credit management.

The role of credit management

Credit management can no longer be seen as simply an administrative task added on to the financial process. Effective and proactive credit management is an essential corporate tool in today's high-speed economy. It completes the cycle of commerce and binds customers to your organization.

Modern credit management is a proactive process of communication that involves the whole of your organization. The credit manager fulfils a central role in initiating and monitoring this process but it is often the effectiveness of your internal communication and the availability of information that are key factors for success.

The reasons for failure

There are a number of reasons why credit management can fail. The involvement of the executive management and the organization as a whole is a vital prerequisite. The fact that many organizations still view credit management as essentially an exercise needed for the annual presentation to the Board can also result in failure. Whilst this is important, it is also essential not to lose sight of other areas of activity that make the credit management process sustainable: such as ensuring appropriate monitoring structures to oversee the credit management process, using the output from the process to shape focused internal credit management activity and using credit management information to inform strategic decision-making, the allocation of resources and business planning activities.

Credit management strategy often remains static year on year as a result of insufficient oversight and challenge from many Boards and Executive Management. This lack of involvement indicates that credit management is being viewed as a compliance requirement and not a business-critical activity.

Profitable credit management

This chapter aims to introduce its readers to the results of recent research conducted among Credit Management professionals. The findings of this survey teach us more about what opportunities are being missed by many credit managers and organizations. What changes in priorities are needed in order to yield the desired improvements at your company? Based on tried and tested experience in credit management we have listed eight major tips to make your credit management profitable.

Challenges and non-payment

Many large companies have recently announced that they will be paying their bills later. There is also a lot of discussion about the payment periods adopted by public bodies. Governments are promising to take steps in this regard. Meanwhile, suppliers to these companies must wait for payment. And that costs a lot of money. In order to still get the invoices paid on time, companies are quick to reach for heavy-handed methods such as using a collection agency. There is then a risk of damaging the relationship with the customer.

Another risk arising from a poorly managed credit management policy (or debtor policy) is non-payment, which can cause liquidity problems for your company. Even more threatening to the survival of your business are bankruptcies. Without a clear insight, good predictions, an insight into trends and a well-thought-out policy companies run the risk of becoming the victim themselves of the bankruptcy of an important customer, resulting in a domino effect. What can organizations do to protect against these sorts of risk? Is it a good idea to go along with major customers' payment demands or to stick to one's own policy?

Good credit management prevents a large number of problems and costs and helps provide your organization with the requisite cash flow. But credit management is about more than just aiming for cash flow. This is precisely the time when one should be thinking about structural improvements to the credit management policy and processes. It is up to the Board and Executive Management to drive through this policy. The economic crisis is an excellent opportunity to place credit management at the top of the list of priorities.

What priorities are required: eight tips

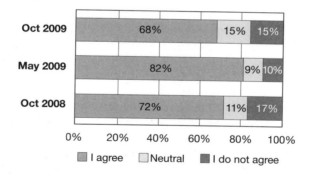

Figure 3.1.1 Confidence in organization's non-payment risk reduction action

The number of credit managers who are confident that their organization is doing enough to reduce the risk of non-payment has fallen considerably over the past six months, as identified in Figure 3.1.1. In the beginning half of 2009, 82 per cent were still confident; the figure has now fallen to 68 per cent. More can and must be done to bring credit management to the desired level.

1. Create structure and focus

Focus in credit management is essential. Determine your risks and put your efforts where the risks are.

Ready for the next level?

Money is the fuel for every business. That's why cash flow and a lower DSO are so important. OnGuard goes even further: smart software, experienced consultants and full support create significant financial and operational advantages. So follow more than 850 clients in more than 25 countries and select a higher gear for your credit management.

OnGuard

Taking credit management to the next level

OnGuard Nederland B.V.

T +31 (0)294 256 666 www.onguard.com/en

The Credit Management solution that pays off

The credit crunch initiated many challenges and more than ever all eyes are focused on working capital. The position and role of the credit manager has grown tremendously. How can you contribute to get control over your company's working capital and how can you manage your credit management effectively and profitably?

OnGuard offers credit management software and services that provide tangible financial and operational benefits. For over ten years we have been supplying credit management solutions to both local and international customers, in large and complex credit management environments, as well as in small and medium sized enterprises.

By implementing OnGuard your collections team will maximise its efficiency and productivity. In addition a reduced DSO, improved cash-flow and reduced interest costs contribute directly to your financial results and the stability of your organisation.

Our "best of breed" application is globally accepted as a credit management solution by more than 850 businesses and 6,000 daily users in over 25 countries.

To find out more about our credit management solutions, visit **www.onguard.com**
or contact Maarten de Wild
via **+31(0)294-256 666** or info@onguard.com

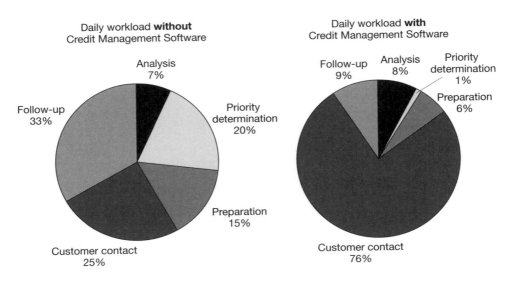

Figure 3.1.2 Daily workload

2. Develop customer management strategies

Credit management software is designed to shape and regulate credit management and query management processes. The customer, the organization and its employees all profit from improved communication, productivity and professionalism. From extensive practical experience we know that many operations are still carried out manually. By using the right tools credit management can focus on 'management by exception' and automate regular activities. The time available for direct customer contact will increase significantly and improve the customer relationship.

Operational activities that take up much of your time can be enormously reduced through the right software structuring. Without the right structure you can easily spend 75 per cent of your time on priority determination, analysis, preparation and follow-up, leaving only 25 per cent for customer contact. Specialized credit management software can help you to turn your time allocation around to 75 per cent customer contact, because you will then only need to spend a quarter of your time on preparation and analysis. Research among credit managers has shown that personal contact and a good relationship with the customer are perceived to be the most effective strategy; 63 per cent of credit managers agree with this. However, it is noteworthy that changes to the debtor policy consist less of personal contact with the customer now (68 per cent) than previously (78 per cent). Credit managers therefore see what should be done, but are not doing it sufficiently themselves. We can conclude from this that it is crucial to structure activities correctly. This will make time available to spend on the essential contact with the customer. The most effective strategies are listed in Figure 3.1.3.

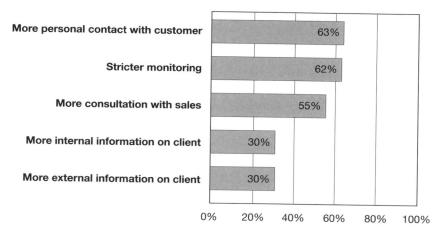

Figure 3.1.3 The most effective customer management strategies

In recent months, many companies have placed greater emphasis on liquidity. That is a good development, but it is not enough. Credit management is about more than just looking at the payment of bills. This is precisely the time when one should be thinking about a structural improvement in policy and processes and then acting on it. The awareness is there, but only a limited number of executives have the nerve to actually invest in it. Credit insurance or handing over invoices to collection agencies sooner are short-term stopgaps. Of course they work, but structural solutions like the use of credit management software are missing. Executives should put credit management high on the agenda in a structured way. Since the relationship with the customer is at the heart of good credit management, this will not only result in cash in the short term, but also considers the long term.

3. Communicate about complaints

A good example of where things can go wrong in terms of communication is the handling of complaints. If you are dissatisfied about supplied products or services, you want to have it resolved before you pay the invoice for them. It is particularly frustrating if complaints are not being dealt with properly, but reminders are still arriving. Rapid and personal handling of a complaint, which is an important element within credit management, ensures that customers move to payment more rapidly and are left feeling positive. Personal, direct and effective communications about invoices ensure improved relationships with customers. Another aspect of good credit management policy is that it helps create greater efficiency and improves the internal processes. Not only does this lead to cost savings, but it also prevents annoyances like duplicated reminders, overlooked invoices and unnecessary turmoil.

4. Go to customers

Credit managers and CFOs need to go out to customers with the salespeople. Only then will you get the right information and the correct insight into the customer, which will mean that you can help the customer with paying your outstanding invoices. Talk to the customer about payment periods and invoicing. You can hear a lot from a customer: what is happening within the company, within the chain, within the sector. Maybe a couple of amended agreements can limit the risks for all the parties.

5. Work from your own knowledge

Ratings and risk scores do not provide sufficient information, particularly not in the current unstable market. The position today might have changed completely in a month's time; your experiences may be different from those of the market, as recorded in Figure 3.1.4.

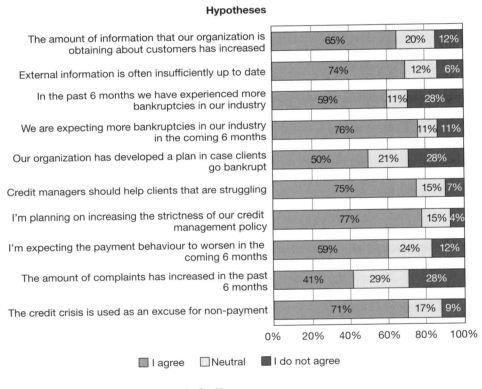

Figure 3.1.4 OnGuard research findings

In our research, 65 per cent of credit managers confirmed that they have started obtaining more information about customers. Unfortunately, 74 per cent feel that this external information is insufficiently up to date.

Avoiding payment problems is more and more dependent on your own knowledge and expertise. That is far more valuable than outside information. You can gain a better insight into the payment behaviour of customers with the right data, which will allow you to anticipate future trends. Executives must base themselves firmly on their own information, if this is available to a high enough quality level. And there is a shortage of this at some companies. Executives like to rely on figures, but will also have to learn to assess risks better themselves. As an executive it is worth looking ahead instead of steering on the basis of past figures; and not just figures, but also trends in payment behaviour.

It is therefore important to gather and analyse valuable information about payment behaviour yourself. Credit management software often offers the opportunity to access the right information very easily and quickly.

6. Give your credit manager space

Your credit manager's 'gut feeling' and expertise are very useful in this regard. It is vital that attention is paid to their position and status within the organization. Not only do executives need to realize this, but credit managers also need to start taking on that role. In most organizations credit managers fulfil an advisory role in relation to executives. The fact that more and more executives are consulting their credit manager is a good development. Credit managers should become more assertive in order for the advice to be adopted. And they must demand more by providing better underpinning and by taking actual steps to get the cash flow under control in a structured way. The executive must give them this space and be prepared to be open to this.

7. Allow credit managers to participate in thinking about contracts and sales

Your credit manager's expertise can be utilized in many areas. When it comes to preventing problems, it is worth including your credit management department in thinking about new contracts and sales. For example, let the credit manager come along on contract negotiations for new customers in order to agree payment periods and conditions. Use the knowledge that your credit manager has of the sector, the type of customer and their payment behaviour. Let credit managers separate the good customers from the bad. After all, good credit management policy results in effective segmentation of the customer portfolio and is heavily focused on retaining customers and limiting risks. It avoids the risk of the credit management department responding too late and having to chase events. Involving them at an early stage avoids a lot of potential payment problems.

The credit management department can contribute to better sales, particularly in the area of customer acceptance. With customer acceptance and early segmentation you can correctly assess the financial risks and link your individual actions to them. Collaboration between the sales department and the credit management department is more important than ever for a business. Executives must therefore work hard to achieve this.

8. Do not automatically accept a postponement of payment

One trend is that large companies in particular are unilaterally extending their payment period and are settling accounts later, sometimes only after 90 days. They thus keep hold of their money for longer, and you bear the cost. A lot of companies accept this without argument, out of fear of losing the customer. Yet that is not necessary. The rejection is almost always accepted, because agreements have been made. They are simply trying it on, and the vast majority fall for it out of fear. If the major customer starts threatening to depart, do not panic too quickly. Do not accept it, and preferably do not enter into discussions about it either.

If important customers extend their payment periods, then enter into discussions with them. If clear agreements have been made about payments during the sales process, you can fall back on them. The key to the issue lies in the fact that by involving credit management during sales, this sort of confusion is ruled out in advance.

Conclusion

The importance of good credit management is currently becoming clearer than ever. It is up to the Board and Executive Management to give credit management a more important role within the organization. It can be concluded that, despite taking steps and making plans, there are still many opportunities that credit managers are not seizing. The fact that 77 per cent intend to refine their credit management policy further over the coming period appears to confirm this.

Credit managers in turn must raise their profile and demonstrate their added value for the organization. Focusing on good credit management is crucial for many organizations in the current economic climate.

A new generation of financial rating services

Xavier Denecker, Coface – UK & Ireland

Introduction

The credit crunch of 2008, and ensuing worldwide recession from which recovery will be painfully slow for all the developed economies – and particularly the US and UK – illustrated the inadequacy of the conventional data offerings of credit agencies on which commerce and industry, as well as insurers, had previously depended.

Setting aside the high-risk strategies and bad judgements of secondary mortgage providers and banks trading in complex financial instruments – which came close to causing the collapse of the global financial system – the damage caused by poor credit information to companies both large and small through the deep recession that followed cannot be exaggerated. In tough times, where cash flow is crucial, prompt and reliable current information on the creditworthiness and financial stability of customers, suppliers and service providers is of paramount importance.

At the levels of country risk rating, international trade and listed companies, the services of the major credit rating agencies, of which Standard & Poor's, Moody's and Fitch dominate, came under scrutiny after their failure to predict performance in the early stages of the financial crisis. One year later in the United States, where these three companies account for 98 per cent of listed company ratings among the

10 approved by the Securities and Exchange Commission (SEC), the SEC is taking steps to introduce new rules to oversee and regulate the ratings industry with a raft of new initiatives.

In the case of listed companies that are required to file regular financial reports, the information is sufficient in most cases to make a reliable assessment of credit-worthiness in times of relative economic stability. However, in times of economic downturn or recession, the risk of unexpected events and rapid balance sheet or liquidity deterioration are heightened and re-assessment using this method may not be timely.

At the secondary level, where credit data is generated locally on unlisted compa-nies, other businesses and individuals, the quality of information is of greater concern, even in calmer conditions of steady economic growth. In the UK, for example, company accounts filed at Companies House are often out of sync with reality because the system does not demand rapid reporting. Audited accounts for the previous year now take nine months before being available and the abbreviated accounts, which are seldom required to be audited for SMEs, do not provide suffi-cient information necessary for detailed assessment. In some other EU jurisdictions the problem is more acute. In Germany, for example, where confidentiality of finan-cial information takes precedence, private limited companies do not always respect the obligation of filing accounts for public inspection. These problems are endemic but have been exacerbated by the tumult of the past two years with an increased need for reliable, current and more rapidly updated financial information.

Better practice in financial ratings

Transparency and dialogue

Companies are the biggest bankers for their client companies – of every £5 of short-term credit granted to a business, £1 comes from banks and £4 from suppli-ers. Therefore, all suppliers need to decide to whom and how much they grant credit, and who they ask for cash payments. They can either decide this alone or with the help of a partner, such as a business information provider, credit insurer or a financing company.

In order to improve dialogue with companies and share financial management information to enhance the quality of financial ratings – and ultimately contribut-ing to maintaining confidence between companies throughout the world – Coface implemented a Transparency Charter in April 2009. This Charter is available to the 130,000 Coface clients and their customers, thereby reaching out to millions of companies. By registering, they will access their Coface rating and its evolution, free of charge; and they will be able to confidentially correct or complete Coface's information on their company.

This may involve accessing a Coface score ('what is the probability of the company honouring all its payment commitments in the coming 12 months?') or a Coface credit opinion ('based on the information available, what is a reasonable amount of credit to extend?'). Coface is well aware of its responsibilities and in implementing the Transparency Charter (see Figure 3.2.1) is helping all companies to manage a vital asset: an image of financial solidity.

Coface commits to:

1. Inform all Coface clients or their customers of their own Coface rating and their credit opinion (all free of charge and on simple request);
2. Transmit any reassessment of their Coface ratings or credit opinions (free of charge);
3. Check with companies the veracity and severity of any payment incidents concerning them and of which Coface is aware, prior to making any decisions;
4. Analyse in a fully confidential manner all financial information that a company sends to Coface before such information becomes public and to inform the company of any impact that such information might have on ratings prior to making any decisions.

Figure 3.2.1 The Coface transparency charter

Coface global @rating system

During the first decade of the 21st century, Coface, the French credit insurer and credit agency, has emerged at the forefront of the international credit insurance industry. Ranked third after Euler Hermes and Atradius as a credit insurer, Coface now has an annual turnover of €1.6 billion, operating worldwide in more than 60 countries.

Coface originated as a domestic export credit agency after the Second World War and provided outsourcing solutions for credit to French exporters. The opening up and expansion of the European Union in the 1990s stimulated the group's international expansion.

The @rating system is designed to assess the capacity of companies to meet their financial obligations towards customers and suppliers. There are several assessment tools available:

■ @rating scores are calculated on a statistical basis for all buyers present in the Coface database. They are on a scale of 0 to 10, each position being associated with a probability of default.
■ @rating credit opinions identify the recommended credit exposure for a company using a very simple scale of five rating levels, each corresponding to a fixed value. The service can be customized to indicate a specific amount if required.

@rating credit opinions are available for over 50 million companies worldwide and this information is used by Coface when assessing credit risk, thus reflecting its expertise in both business information and credit insurance.

■ Country @ratings support international trade and commerce by enhancing the security of transactions. They are available on 165 countries and are one of Coface's key areas of expertise.

The Country @ratings measure the average level of short-term non-payment risk presented by companies in a particular country. It reflects the extent to which a country's economic, financial and political outlook influences financial commitments of local companies.

The Country @rating is based on three factors:

1. the country's economic, political and financial outlook, such as economic and government fiscal vulnerabilities and weaknesses in relation to the geopolitical environment (eg risks of a foreign currency liquidity crisis, external over-indebtedness or weaknesses in the banking sector);
2. the business climate;
3. average company payment behaviour.

Coface has developed a seven-grade classification ranging from A1 through to A4 for investment grade risks and B, C and D for below investment grade risks. Summaries of the country @rating data and assessments can be accessed without charge on the Coface websites: www.Coface.com and www.trading-safely.com.

■ Business climate ratings provide an assessment of the overall quality of a given country's business environment. Specifically, they reflect the availability and reliability of corporate financial information, whether the legal system provides fair and efficient creditor protection and whether a country's institutional framework is favourable for companies. The business climate rating system, which is one of the three components of country @ratings, uses the same seven-step scale.
■ Sector @ratings measure the average level of default risk associated with companies in particular sectors. Each rating evaluates the likely impact on short-term payment behaviour of economic prospects and the average corporate financial situation in a given sector. To determine Sector ratings, Coface combines three measurements:
   – the vulnerability of economic conditions in the sector, which reflects the influence of market prospects, price levels and production costs on company solvency;
   – the company's financial solidity in the sector, which reflects the capability of companies to cope with economic downturns;
   – the payment experience on transactions payable in the short-term as reflected by the Coface databases.

Coface establishes Sector @ratings on 10 levels ranging from A+ for the lowest risks to D for the highest.

The new Coface financial rating

What the market needs in 2010

The rapid deterioration in country economies, business climates and conditions during 2008 and 2009 has affected sectors and companies with varying severity. Similar disparities will arise during the phases of recovery in each country and sector, for which forecast timing and rates of recovery differ widely. Just as 2008 balance sheets were inadequate during the downturn for credit assessment purposes where some corporate turnovers had declined from 30 to 50 per cent, so too will 2009 balance sheets be an unsatisfactory basis for the credit ratings of companies and sectors staging strong recoveries.

Balanced assessment demands evidence of the real situation with ratings for Stock Exchange listed companies and unlisted private companies based on a continuous flow of information at moderate cost. Realistic information and ratings are needed by insurance companies to set their premium rates, by banks providing asset-based finance and, more widely, by those engaged in industry and commerce both domestically and internationally. Ratings based on transparency and certification, are also an essential requirement for successful company flotation.

What the new financial rating provider offers:

Coface solely provides corporate ratings, which, in the financial sector, act as a safeguard against badly controlled diversification into the rating of complex financial instruments. More widely, many companies can benefit from the Coface rating service, which is both statistically reliable and cost-effective.

The Coface financial rating is calculated based on an internal score and is associated with a probability of default. It abides with strict criteria of quality, including permanent monitoring and periodical contact to the rated companies' management. The rating provides an assessment of the financial stability of a company and is based on the probability of payment default within the next 12 months.

Summary

Coface's strategy as the only provider in the market to provide a holistic credit management service is to offer the following solutions:

- Trade Credit Insurance – protection against insolvency and risk of payment default.
- Receivables Finance – flexible financing to boost cash flow.
- A unique combination of Protection and Finance provided by an integrated credit insurer and receivables financier.

- Intelligent Credit Analysis – Coface Ratings, opinions, scores and Business information.
- Receivables Management services and the collection of outstanding payments.

The cycle of Coface's credit management service is illustrated in Figure 3.2.2 below.

Figure 3.2.2 The credit management wheel

This full suite of solutions means that companies can use the approved insurable credit limits and cover to set their general credit policies and credit terms for customers and suppliers individually. They can identify and define their exposure to risk in selecting suppliers and deciding whether the credit demands of their customers are acceptable or too much, and whether the account should be maintained.

By offering a complete business-to-business trade credit solution, Coface's holistic approach to credit management offers its clients greater flexibility, security and ultimately peace of mind.

Every day, 130,000 companies call on Coface's expertise in its four business lines (Trade Receivables Protection, Trade Receivables Finance, Rating and Business Information and Trade Receivables Management) for the purposes of managing their inter-company credit.

Note: Visit www. Coface.com to access the full range of Coface services.

For more effective communications solutions.

Deliver the right message, to the right people, at the right time.

Our automated interactive voice messaging solution adds value to your collections strategy, allowing you to get to know your debtor.

Use TALKINGtech to segment your customers - gain intelligence on the best contact methods and feed those results back into your CRM system and your collections strategy.

Use our knowledge of the credit industry combined with the latest in automated voice technology, and you've got a powerful debtors management tool.

For further information call **020 7987 0101** or visit **www.talkingtech.com**

TALKINGtech
the voice of your business

The new ways to contact debtors

Shaun Maloney, TALKINGtech

The use of technology-driven debtor contact methodologies has seen a dramatic increase over the last three years. No longer are collections departments constrained to letters and outbound-calling strategies. Automated technologies such as interactive voice messaging (IVM), email and SMS are now being used on an ever-increasing level to augment or replace traditional contact strategies.

Without a doubt, the United States pioneered automation in outbound contact. In the 1980s and 1990s it was common to receive robotic telephone calls selling double glazing, carpet cleaning or advising you that you had been 'chosen as the lucky winner'.

It is no surprise that the US market has since implemented regulations to restrict automated-contact technologies and protect the public from persistent unsolicited marketing calls and spamming, and these regulations are now being replicated in other markets.

However, the benefit of such regulation is that contact technologies are now being used strategically and responsibly, gaining acceptance within the credit and collections industry worldwide and, more importantly, legitimacy with government regulators.

In September 2008, OFCOM, the UK communications regulator, released a statement officially recognizing voice messaging as a legitimate contact method and its clear public benefit.

Public acceptance of IVM

The biggest change in recent years has been seen in the public acceptance of alternative contact methods and their value as opposed to the various letters and outbound-calling strategies traditionally employed by most credit and collections departments.

In 2007 an independent survey company canvassed debtor customers of a large telecom provider within the United Kingdom who had been contacted via automated IVM. Nearly three-quarters of all those surveyed thought that it was a very good idea, contributing to a total positive opinion base of 86 per cent.

The survey results showed that few consumers would prefer being contacted by a real person. In most cases this was because consumers were embarrassed to speak to a real person about their debt, with many, in fact, considering a person-to-person discussion about their debt to be potentially confrontational.

Additionally, consumers surveyed appreciated having some advance warning of, and choice about, speaking to a real person, which was afforded them by IVM.

Why choose voice messaging?

The motivation for introducing automated contact methods within the credit and collection industry do not vary much from company to company.

For both the mature and emerging country markets it is about reducing cost of collection and speed of contact – reaching the right party quicker, and so prompting payment ahead of other debts in the consumer's mailbox. In the current economic climate, smaller credit and collections teams operating under increased pressure to collect earlier in the collection cycle continue to look for direct debtor contact methods that emulate the human contact in engagement and a debtor-prompted cure outcome.

For emerging markets and new adopters of this technology, where contact centre seats are more affordable, a key driver is the ability of credit and collections teams to be more targeted in their debtor contact strategies.

For instance, the South African market has poor mail delivery rates, but one of the highest mobile phone penetration rates globally; hence the extensive use of text messaging as a contact method.

Unfortunately, this market also suffers from 85 per cent of mobile phones being prepaid with a 45 per cent number-churn rate per annum, which creates a challenge for right party contact. Applying automated technologies to scenarios such as this can provide cost-effective scale and targeted delivery within the collections process.

Instant feedback

The common theme across all companies and countries is the drive by credit and collections teams to become more targeted without adding complexity and cost.

Unlike traditional contact methods, automated technologies provide instant feedback to identify the most effective contact method at an individual debtor level. What worked last time and what did not?

The increased use of automated technologies within the credit and collections industry results in reduced operational resource, lower cost-per-pound or dollar collected and reduced bad debt churn.

Know your debtors

It is standard practice for companies to apply a risk score to a new customer upon their acquisition. The more flexible CRM and billing systems even allow for the revision and reclassification of risk scores during the customer life cycle.

These risk scores are often based on spend value and method of payment; accordingly, they fit in nicely with debt-provisioning rules. But what is the value of the risk score once the customer enters the collections process? Do the assumptions on which a risk score is given at acquisition have any relevance to the customer's propensity to pay? What is more, does it provide any value in assessing the most appropriate contact strategy for that debtor? By appropriate I mean cost and result effective.

Learn about your customer

Learning about debtors – and not just the information that is sitting on a finance or lease agreement – is about taking information and overlaying it with external factors that may be affecting that person at that time. Essentially, you are looking at it from their position, such as employment status and changes for that sector, trends in household affordability and debt levels.

This level of granular debtor segmentation and the application of propensity-to-pay score is fast becoming a must-have within the blue-chip finance and utility sectors. The debt collection market is no stranger to geo-demographic mapping, or debtor segmentation, having applied the science for some time now in the valuation of debt portfolios pre-purchase.

Just as critical in the exercise of knowing your debtor is what you can learn about them at an individual level. This involves the continual updating of your debtors' responses, reactions and interaction with collections methods once they have entered that collections cycle.

Promise to pay – making them count

The worth of a debtor's promise-to-pay (PTP) can be influenced by their payment history, cultural factors and understanding of the consequences of non-payment. We all know how it goes: the call centre collections agent is in discussion with the debtor, with the result that the debtor promises to make a payment in the next couple of days. A fairly acceptable arrangement for lower risk, early-stage collections. If the debtor subsequently carries through on the payment, great; if not, ongoing actions within the collections process mean wasting valuable time. The debtors will be more likely to be increasingly evasive of further collections methods, the result being an increase in the cost of collection.

Understand your debtors' history

It goes without saying that the first step in avoiding PTP disappointments is understanding the debtor history. Historical broken promise is the obvious indicator, and, increasingly, billing and collections systems are providing for this level of management information. This historical debtor reporting can be overlaid with other factors, such as debtor-customer tenure, spending pattern and payment method, providing for debtor segmentation. This allows for targeted debtor treatment within the collections process that is most likely to succeed.

One factor influencing collections methodology and strategy that is increasingly overlooked within the United Kingdom is that of the debtor's culture. In an ever-increasingly multicultural country, where English may not be the debtor's first language, collections agents can easily be taken in by the mañana (Spanish for 'tomorrow') approach.

We can all recount stories of relaxed holidays abroad where the prevailing attitude is very much 'why do something today when it can be done tomorrow'. Great on holiday, but not the attitude you want from your debtor.

Adding this debtor's language preference to debtor segmentation rules can provide the opportunity to engage the debtor in their language of choice and in a manner that carries greater meaning and understanding.

Clearly, it would be unrealistic to think that collections departments have large language skill and resource within their teams. However, using automated-messaging technology to engage the debtor in their language of choice as a first contact point can then result in the debtor understanding the issue without it being lost in translation. Resolution can then be achieved by the debtor being transferred to a language skill group within a collections team, receiving confirmations of promises, terms and conditions or contact details automatically by text message; once again in their language of choice and terms that are meaningful.

What are the consequences?

The most important influence on follow-through is the debtor's understanding of the consequences of non-payment and the value they put on them. It is of little use to send written confirmation to a debtor of their PTP when the letter arrives three days after the PTP due date has passed. In fact, such actions can have the effect of providing the debtor with a further excuse to delay payment. Apart from this, the process of sending collections letters can add to the cost of collection, with little benefit other than a record of the conversation. The quicker the confirmation of a PTP and the consequences of not making payment can reach the debtor, the higher the probability the debtor will make the payment.

Follow up with your debtors

We provided a large multinational utility company with a direct contact collections strategy providing automated outbound messaging with resulting PTP confirmations by text message directly after the call. It had some startling results. The debtors who made a promise-to-pay, and received a text message confirming their commitment, were up to three times more likely to honour their commitment than those who made a promise and did not receive a reminder text message.

Of those who did honour their commitment, 70 per cent who received a text message made payment within three days, with 20 per cent making payment the very same day. This compared to a return of 40 per cent of honoured commitments from customers without a text message follow-up, and only five per cent of those customers paying on the same day. The debtor self-cure rate substantially increased as the text message PTP confirmation provided the amount to pay and number where the debtor could make their automated payment.

Welcome calls – the credit process starts here

There are benefits of welcome calls in the debt prevention area; however, the age-old argument comes up. How much will this cost in time and resource and who will pay for it?

Invariably, customer service departments are asked to pick up the cost. They will argue that they are too busy taking reactive inbound calls to make proactive outbound calls, which will predominantly benefit credit and collections departments. And they do not have the budget anyway.

Credit and collections teams will argue they are too busy dealing with customers that owe money to worry about those that do not as yet; and they do not have the budget anyway. So the end result is that welcome calls may get an occasional burst from a small team in customer service, but come to a grinding halt when budget or time gets squeezed.

But welcome calls need not be expensive, complicated or draining of resources.

As a case study, a large national shop-front finance company undertakes welcome calls using automated outbound messaging. The outbound greets and verifies, and Data Protection Act checks the right party using interactive voice messaging. The customer is greeted as a new and valued client; then the service proceeds to validate all the five key customer details as described above.

At any point the customer can opt to speak to the call centre live agent. The benefit is that the point at which they choose to transfer decides the call centre location and skill group they will speak to. As an example, if the customer wishes to change or add to contact details, or discuss a service or product issue, they transfer to the customer service department. If they have a query over their method of payment, direct debit or first bill, they transfer to the credit call centre.

The key in this case is that both the customer service and credit departments share the resource for a shared benefit. And the cost, around 30p per customer contact, is shared.

A welcome call campaign then can be a key tool to reduce the volume of customers entering the credit and collections cycle two or three months into their relationship.

Summary – new contact strategies

No longer are collections departments constrained to letters, outbound dialling and versions thereof. Interactive automated voice messaging, e-mail and SMS are now being used on an ever-increasing level to augment or replace traditional contact strategies.

The rapid increase in these contact methods has been driven by their general market acceptance, companies' drive to reduce cost of collection and the now smaller credit and collections teams looking to be more proactive. The potential risk with these newer technology contact methods is that, over time, they too will become static within collections process and lose their edge, as debtors become familiar with them.

What interactive automated voice messaging, e-mail and SMS provide is the ability to understand and implement the most effective contact method for that debtor base. If the collections process does not or cannot take into account customer propensity to pay, the result will be wasted operational resource, higher cost per pound collected and bad-debt churn.

Improve your cash-flow!

- Your invoices paid faster
- Reduce bad debt
- Improve customer relations
- Reduce administration

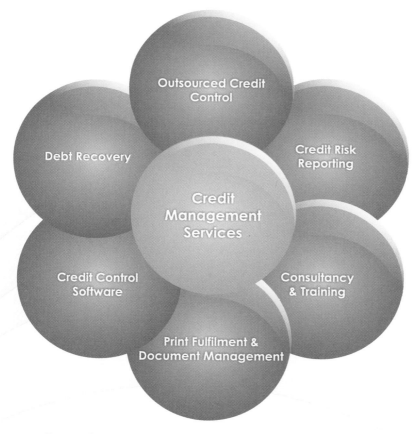

Boost your bottom-line performance!

0207 1005978

www.tak-outsourcing.com

An overview to improving cash flow

Simon Hampton, TAK-Outsourcing Limited

Cash is king, if you had a pound for every time you had heard this old truism you probably wouldn't be reading this!

The purpose of this chapter is to give an overview of a practical approach to assessing your current Credit Control processes, some ideas for reviewing and, if needed, enhancing existing process or designing new processes. Naturally, I tend to favour outsourcing; however, the approach will work for in-house delivery as well as outsourcing and also a hybrid of the two where an outsourcer is engaged alongside an internal team to provide cover for part of a ledger.

Most, if not all business leaders know that cash is the lifeblood of a healthy business. With commercial life being so demanding, finding time to focus upon good process and procedures to collect cash effectively often gets overlooked. When the economy is booming, high-order levels cover and compensate for flaws in Credit Management process much like a puddle will cover the cracks in the pavement; however as the puddle dries, the cracks that can trip up a business appear, sometimes with disastrous results. Many good, profitable businesses have gone bust due to lack of cash.

Poor cash flow as a result of poor Credit Management and Credit Control Process is avoidable. With some time spent and an understanding of best practice, mixed with a dose of pragmatism, process can be improved to deliver dramatic, positive results. Where time is an issue, engaging expert help to analyse, design and in some cases deliver a new process is becoming increasingly popular.

If your collections function is performing well, a review can still uncover areas for improvement. Reducing an already good DSO (Day Sales Outstanding), a measure of the average time it takes for a customer to pay your invoice, even by a seemingly small amount, can yield big benefits particularly for larger businesses.

However you decide to execute your final strategy, the following areas need to be addressed in any review and redesign:

- approach and scope of review;
- credit policy;
- collection strategy;
- collection process;
- escalation and debt recovery;
- implementation of change;
- how to outsource.

Approach and scope

Using a methodical approach is a must; start with a project definition. Examine the data available to help define the issues you wish to address and the scope of your review. Some issues faced by collections teams have their roots in the sales process; therefore sales involvement will probably be needed. Ensure that this initial phase includes mapping the stakeholders, which will help when planning implementation.

The start point will always be some measurement and analysis of your current process performance. This is the result that your current process is producing and will act as a benchmark against which you will measure the effectiveness of any change to process. It may also help decide how far upstream you venture.

The limits of your data will probably depend upon how sophisticated current policy and process is. With a simple process, such as the ruler and highlighter pen (taking the debtors list on a regular basis and highlighting the big numbers that are easy to collect) there will be little data available: generally the overall DSO vs credit terms, the amount of bad debt and the bad debt write-off.

At the other end of the scale, there may be a clear credit policy against which you can measure adherence and more sophisticated processes in place enabling data to be collected upon different sections of the ledger, for example by customer turnover, invoice size, trading record or customer behavior to name a few. This will enable the definition phase to be more precise, homing in on specific areas that are critical to the effectiveness of the process and therefore to be considered for improvement.

Data relating to the regularity with which the task is performed should also be easy to collect. Consistent performance of credit control tasks is a characteristic of a high-performing process.

You will be where you are, and if you are at the stage of no formalized or documented credit policy and credit control process, then that is the start point.

Based upon this analysis, the design of a new process can begin using data gathered regarding reasons for non-payment to help. Map out the steps that will be taken and a timetable for the performance of the tasks – when and how often Credit Control will be carried out. Resource will also be a consideration at this point. Look at the internal resource available and alternate resourcing options such as the use of temps and of course outsourcing. If outsourcing is to be considered, it is a good idea to engage with potential suppliers early as they will be able to help with and, in some cases, conduct much of the work for you.

Have a test phase built into the project to ensure the new policies and processes actually work in practice. Ensure that the process design addresses and, where possible removes barriers to payment within your credit terms. It is far less disruptive to try, fail and adjust on a small-scale project and finalizing a process before communication and roll out. If this is done, then the data from the test can be used as part of the change process to gain the buy-in of the stakeholders.

The aims will vary with each situation; however, the end result should encompass the following elements.

Credit policy

This is a point for careful consideration. Credit Control must not become a sales prevention department; imposing a credit policy so strict that bad debt is reduced by virtue of doing no business. Conversely, a policy that is too loose will have sales romping away doing business with anyone and everyone regardless of their ability to pay.

For new customers, there should be a defined process for account opening, including some form of credit checking. There are several online services that can provide data to help assess a customer's creditworthiness. Based upon this, a credit limit should be set to minimize trading risk. The account opening process should ensure that all required information is collected regarding new customers. It's amazing how often credit is provided without knowing the legal entity to which it is actually being provided.

Once a customer is on-board, ongoing credit checks should take place at regular intervals, dependent on the level of risk with the account. You'll probably wish to increase credit limits for regular clients with a proven history. The health of your customers will vary with time; it is important that early warning signs are spotted to reduce the exposure to company failure. Credit-checking services are now available that integrate seamlessly with your accounts system to provide real-time risk-indicators relating to your customers and the level of credit provided to them.

Collection strategy

Depending upon your start point, the strategy will focus upon areas of the ledger that need intervention to improve cash flow. You may need to categorize your customers to allow different collection processes to be used; for example, between key clients and those that order from you on an ad hoc basis. Each collection strategy should be appropriate to the customer group and easily implemented and adhered to.

Once the collection processes have been defined for each group they should be used in a consistent manner. Your customers will become accustomed to your collection process and will improve their payment habits in response.

Collection process

The process map should be time bound from the payment due date and detail each task and the responsible person and business area. A flow diagram is a good way of publishing this as it is easy to detail the core process and dispute and query resolution loops.

The process used will be dependent on the category of customer and size of the invoice. For example, with larger invoice values you may carry out a courtesy call at a set point after the invoice is sent to ensure that there are no disputes and that it is on track for authorization. Where possible the contacts should be personal in order to build a relationship with your customer at payment level. It's often the case that the credit control team has more contact with your customer than sales; so they can be important in improving customer relations. E-mails are useful to confirm points agreed on the phone and may be used as part of an automated collection process for invoices of smaller value. Letters can be used as part of the escalation process and often have a stronger effect than e-mails; for example, as a final demand or warning that your customer may be passed to a debt recovery agency.

At every stage, records need to be kept detailing content of conversations and disputes or queries that have been addressed. This helps build a customer profile, and history can be invaluable if a debt needs to be passed to debt recovery or legal process.

Escalation

Despite your best efforts, some customers will still owe you money at the end of the Credit Control process. Documenting the consequences is important as it will ensure a consistent approach to delinquent payers. Done properly this will help educate and improve speed of payment where late payment is due to customer behaviour.

It is important to bear in mind that there are some customers that a business is better off without. Having rules in place will force a case to be built for continuing to trade with a consistently delinquent customer.

Debt recovery

There are many debt recovery agencies and quality varies considerably. Those offering the lowest rates (or 'free service' whereby the agency retains late payment fees from the debtor) may not end up being the most cost effective as they may operate a restricted process of letter and limited number of calls before escalation to legal process, which tends to be expensive. As with most things, you get what you pay for. An agency with a realistic rate may achieve a higher collection rate without the need for legal action and, importantly, may provide you with intelligence-based advice as to whether a debtor is worth pursuing with legal process. Transparency is also important when dealing with a collection agency; ensure that reporting is clear and accurate and that payments from your debtors will be passed over to your account promptly

Implementation of change

Once your new policies and procedures are designed, tested and documented, an implementation plan needs to be considered. Although it is important to implement and embed the changes, it need not be over-complex. In short, to be successful it should ensure that all the people affected by and responsible for elements in the new process are clear about the reasons for change, the business benefits and their role and responsibilities with the new process.

If outsourcing is a feature of the new Credit Control provision, then ensure that contracting is done with care. If the business is new to outsourcing, then the areas identified below need to be included in consideration and selection of service providers.

Successful outsourcing

The following steps will help keep you out of trouble.

Clarity

Accuracy and detail on both sides will help ensure that both parties' expectations are understood and met from outset. Ensure that you describe very carefully the work you expect the outsourcer to perform on your behalf and agree who is responsible for each aspect of the process. Make sure the outsourcer understands and describes how their service meets your needs as they describe the operation of the service. Remember you are delegating responsibility and risk, as you would to an employee. You will still ultimately be responsible for your business.

Take a reference

Speak to some current customers of your prospective partners and check any claims made by prospective outsourcing suppliers. One is a minimum; three is probably enough. Check for consistent stories and any common errors and try to verify any claims made by the potential suppliers.

Transition plan

Ask your potential partners to draw up a plan to move from your current situation to the outsourced situation. This need not be over-complex, but does need to include relevant milestones:

Operational plan

Document roles; responsibilities; planned communication. Where an activity is time-bound, a clear process map detailing dependencies and deadline needs, signed off by both parties should be included.

Contracting

Legal support from a firm with relevant experience is advisable. Suppliers will generally use standard documentation. Ensure that this provides adequate remedies should the service fail significantly; inclusion of a dispute resolution procedure that enables service to continue for enough time to make alternate arrangements, where a serious failure occurs, can be useful. If you are including service measures, ensure that they are easily managed and don't become an additional burdensome task. If you do target an improvement in DSO, be realistic. What can be achieved will depend upon the start point, that is, how generally delinquent you have allowed your customers to become. If your DSO is way out of kilter it may be possible to make some big improvements very quickly. Our own experience shows this to be the case with several clients; one in particular, a printing company, had not been communicating with customers at all. Invoices were issued and hope was the only strategy from there on. We halved this company's aged debt within three months. Also consider past performance; look at the best figure achieved in the last four years, if it is easy to do so, and give some thought to the level at which you would feel comfortable.

Exit

Plan for exit before you enter into the agreement. Expect to pay a penalty if you wish to cancel for convenience and ensure that you and your chosen supplier are clear and committed to respective responsibilities on expiration or cancellation of the contract.

Outsourcing can be a very cost effective, flexible and scalable tool, freeing up time, avoiding the need to increase headcount, leaving you more able to focus on growing your business.

In summary, whatever you decide to do with credit management, ensure that it is reviewed regularly, that practice adheres to the new policies and processes and that these still match the needs of your business and current market conditions.

Done well your business will be more efficient, will have lower working capital requirements and reduced risk to losses due to company failures, and you will have deeper knowledge of your customers, all of which are good for a healthy, profitable business.

Securing a job in the credit and collections industry

Brett Marlow, Jobs In Credit

For most businesses 2009 was a difficult year and recruitment businesses have perhaps one of the closest insights into how badly the recession is affecting everyday people.

I launched the United Kingdom's only jobs board dedicated to credit recruitment – www.jobsincredit.com – five years ago and have seen a dramatic change in the ways companies look at recruiting new staff as well as the number of roles available. Before September 2008 we had an average of 2,500 live jobs at anytime; throughout most of 2009 this figure has dropped to roughly 700 live jobs. So, now more than ever, candidates need to be extremely well prepared before they start applying for jobs or thinking about attending interviews.

Your CV

We all know that CV writing is a controversial subject – part art, part science – and if you ask any two people what their idea is of the perfect CV, you will no doubt get two different and rather subjective responses. However, in consultation with The CV Centre, we have put together a number of dos, don'ts and common pitfalls on which most personnel professionals will agree. If you bear these in mind when preparing your own CV, you stand a much better chance of surviving the 'CV cull'!

Length

Far too long – probably the single biggest mistake people make when preparing their own CVs. Professional CV reviewers recommend keeping your CV brief and cutting out the waffle. Two pages is generally the maximum, and for those with little experience one page generally makes much more sense. They also use other techniques such as bullet pointing, etc to help make your CV easier to read.

Detail

Eliminate all unnecessary detail. Take a look at each piece of information you are thinking of including and ask 'Does this help my case?' If it doesn't, then you should simply leave it out.

History

Try to concentrate on your recent history and summarize older information. Employers are definitely most interested in your latest achievements and positions.

Interests and activities

A common mistake is to write far too much under this heading. With the CV trend moving increasingly towards the American resumé style, which precludes such a section, you should try to keep it to a minimum.

Professional preparation

Even having taken the above points into account, writing your own CV can often be a daunting and time-consuming task. And it could be said that there really is no substitute for taking advantage of in-depth professional experience.

Job hunting

There are many routes to finding new roles: recruitment agencies, industry magazines and industry associations. As with most things these days, the internet tends to be the first source that people use when looking for a new job and this is where sites such as www.jobsincredit.com become extremely useful.

The advantages that using jobs boards or looking for jobs online offer is the access they provide to the broadest range of roles within your particular niche. Most sites are free to register and use. They usually offer services such as 'jobs by e-mail', allowing you to be notified of the latest jobs as they are added to the site.

The danger of looking for jobs via the internet is that people tend to think that it's quite easy to apply for any role, even if it is obviously outside of their ability and experience. Our advice is to be realistic; read the job description accurately and be honest with yourself as to whether you should be applying for the role. Don't apply for positions to which you are unlikely to be either able or willing to commute, even if you are perfect for the role. If you can't get to it, then you will never get the job.

The interview

Most candidates are understandably nervous about attending job interviews – but nerves can often be a useful tool for sharpening up your performance. However, if your nerves take over to the extent that they interfere with your ability to come across well at interview, then it's clear that you need to calm down. The key to preventing pre-interview jitters is to prepare yourself thoroughly.

Organize yourself

In most cases, you will be notified that you have got through to the interview stage a few days in advance. You can use this time to prepare – and the better prepared you are, the fewer your reasons to be nervous. Try to find out as much as you can about the employer. Reference libraries, your local careers centre and the internet (if you have access) are all good sources of information. You should also read up on the type of work you are applying for. Go over the job description thoroughly and make a note of any questions you would like to ask at the interview.

Travel arrangements

It is vital that you find out:

- Where the employer is based. It seems obvious but if you need to get the train, find out where the nearest railway station is.
- When the interview is to be held. Calculate how long it will take you to get there and make sure that you leave in plenty of time (particularly if you are relying on public transport).
- Where the interview is taking place. If the employer occupies a number of rooms in separate buildings, it is easy to end up in the wrong place.
- What is the name of your contact.
- Who exactly will be interviewing you.

Confidence

Confident people inspire confidence in others. If you appear confident that you are able to do the job, the employer is likely to believe that you can. Naturally it is important not to go to the other extreme and appear over-confident, arrogant or pushy.

Expect the unexpected

Bear in mind that interviews vary enormously. You may be asked to sit an aptitude test or prove that you have the necessary skills for the job – a typing test for example. The interview itself may be a quick, informal chat across a crowded office or it could involve a panel of interviewers all firing questions at you. There may even be group activities with other candidates designed to see how you perform in a team situation, or you may be called back for further interviews on another day. Often, candidates fail to perform to the best of their abilities because they are thrown into a situation they are not expecting. The answer: expect the unexpected. You cannot prepare for every eventuality but you can be aware that the format of the interview may come as a surprise to you. Have faith in your own skills and experience and allow the employer to see you at your best.

Interview questions

Obviously, no one can know exactly what questions they will be asked at interview but there are certain topics that will almost certainly come up. Think through your answers to the following questions beforehand:

- Tell me about your work experience. What did you do, what did you enjoy, what were you good at, why did you leave each job?
- Why have you applied for this job?
- Why do you want to work for this company?
- What can you, above all the other applicants, bring to this job?
- What did you do with your time when you were out of paid employment?

Look good, feel good

Research has shown that your interviewer is likely to make up his or her mind about you within 30 seconds of having met you. Use this. Make sure that you have an outfit that is smart and presentable. It's a good idea to try the whole thing on before the day of the interview to check that there are no drooping hems or buttons missing. It is also worthwhile polishing your shoes – details like this can make all the difference. And, if you feel that you have made an effort and look good, you will appear to be more confident and relaxed.

The big day

Make sure that you allow yourself enough time to get ready and that you have with you all your exam certificates, records of achievement, testimonials and anything else relevant to the job. Also remember to take the letter inviting you to the interview and any maps that you might need. Leave in time to arrive about 10 minutes early for the interview – this will allow you to gather your thoughts, go to the loo, check your appearance, etc. When you arrive, give your name to the receptionist if there is one. Try to relax – everyone gets nervous before interviews. The chances are that you will feel more nervous than you look and anyway, most interviewers are trained to make allowances for the fact that you are likely to be on edge.

First Impressions

The following tips will help you make a positive impression:

- Shake hands firmly (but not to the extent that they require first aid) with all the interviewers when you first enter the room – and smile.
- Maintain eye contact while answering all questions – and remember to speak up.
- Try to avoid 'Yes' and 'No' answers to questions even if they seem appropriate; they tend to be conversation stoppers. Make sure that you answer questions fully without chattering on unnecessarily.
- Never lie at interview or say something that you cannot substantiate, but make sure that you present yourself in the best possible light.
- When you are asked if you have any questions, use this as an opportunity to demonstrate your interest and enthusiasm. Begin with questions about training, other people you will be working with and the job specification. Save questions about pay and holidays until last.
- If you are not asked about something that you feel illustrates an important aspect of your ability to do the job, don't be afraid to bring it up yourself at the end of the interview.
- Make sure that you find out when you can expect to hear whether you have been successful – it could be anything from the same day (in which case, you may be asked to wait around for a decision) to a few days.
- Remember to thank the interviewers for their time before you leave.

The wait

You should hear one way or the other within a week or so of the interview taking place, unless the employer has specified otherwise. If you do not hear within this time, telephone the organization and enquire politely whether a decision has been reached. If you were not successful, try to treat the interview as a learning experience – nearly everybody gets a few setbacks when they are hunting for a new job. Think about why you were not selected and if there was anything that you could have done differently to improve your chances of getting the job. Don't be too hard on yourself. It may simply have been that there was a better qualified or more suitable candidate and that, given your experience and skills, you performed to the best of your abilities. Indeed, sometimes there is so little to choose between candidates that, more than anything, success or failure at interview is down to luck. Above all else, remember: there is a job out there with your name on it and if employers haven't recognized your star quality yet, it's up to you to dazzle them!

When it comes to interviews, people often think 'Well, I'll just turn up and be myself'. Which is fine, but it won't get you the job. You need to plan and prepare for an interview as you are still up against many other applicants, and this is your key opportunity to make an impact. Your CV may get your foot in the door but you're on your own in the interview – and sometimes the most able candidates on paper can really shoot themselves in the foot when they actually get to the interview.

Recruiting staff

The way many companies recruit staff is changing significantly in line with the growth in usage of the internet. Companies realize that cost savings can be made by combining a range of recruitment techniques to help find new staff.

Jobs boards have been around for about 12 years with sites like Stepstone, Monster and Jobsite being the forerunners in the United Kingdom. As general usage of the internet has grown, so has the desire to use sites that are tailored to each individual; therefore the growth in niche jobs boards has been dramatic.

I personally worked in the credit industry for around 10 years before deciding to launch www.jobsincredit.com, which is aimed at only advertising vacancies within the area of credit or collections. In five years, we have registered over 42,000 candidates and received an average of 25,000 visitors a month. We charge a low fixed fee to place an advert onto the site and candidates apply directly to vacancies advertised. Therefore there are no placement fees upon the successful employment of a candidate. A good example of how our service works can be seen below from both a client and candidates perspective.

Testimonial

Online recruitment is a breath of fresh air

When write-off debt recovery specialist JB Debt Recovery decided it needed a new Business Development Executive for England, the company head-quartered in Glasgow opted for a fresh approach to recruitment.

Rather than utilize the services of a headhunter or recruitment consultancy, JB Debt Recovery 'googled it' and found jobsincredit.com, much to the delight of Gavin Ritchie, Sales Director at the Scottish firm:

> When we came across Jobs in Credit it was a breath of fresh air. For years we'd been using recruitment consultancies to find high-level people and paying a substantial commission for them. However, it was becoming an increasingly time-consuming process and we were having to talk to many consultancies to find the quality of candidate and the number of people we wanted. Jobs in Credit only deals with credit professionals, who are looking for new roles within the industry. Furthermore, as it's a website it attracts people from all over the UK, so we were accessing a much larger pool of candidates. We also appeared to attract a better quality of candidate.

Statistics certainly reinforce Mr Ritchie's belief. Those people who register their CV with an online recruitment consultancy, such as Jobs in Credit, have on average better qualifications, experience and skills compared to those who find a new position through other recruitment means.

Louise Marshall, JB Debt Recovery's new Business Development Executive, says:

I'm delighted I registered my CV with Jobs in Credit – I wouldn't have secured this role without it. As the whole process was conducted via e-mail and the internet I was able to fit job hunting into my schedule and it was so quick. With the website matchmaking my CV against opportunities and forwarding my details automatically to companies and roles that appealed it made life so easy for me.

I think we've both won because of Jobs in Credit. JB Debt Recovery saved cost, reduced advertising production and planning costs, and cut down the time it takes to deal with applications. I secured employment with a leading company, in a challenging role with an excellent package that I might not have seen advertised elsewhere. I'd definitely encourage people to use jobsin-credit.com to find their next credit role.

Do you need the services of an HCEO?

To find out what an HCEO can do for you in the recovery of your money judgment or possession order visit the Association's website at www.hceoa.org.uk

hceoa
Responsible Enforcement

Providing a profession service

Vernon Phillips,
High Court Enforcement Officers Association

Introduction

Authorized High Court Enforcement Officers (HCEOs) are responsible for executing the judgments and orders of the High Court in England and Wales. They can also execute County Court judgments over £600 if the creditor so requests, provided the judgment is not regulated under the provisions of the Consumer Credit Act 1974.

Background

The post of High Court Enforcement Officer came into existence in 2004 as the result of provisions contained in the Courts Act 2003. HCEOs are the successors to the Under Sheriffs who were previously appointed annually by the Sheriff to carry out his duties. HCEOs are appointed (authorized) by the Lord Chancellor or his 'designated person' (the Senior Master of the Queen's Bench Division of the High Court) pursuant to paragraph 2(1) of Schedule 7 of the Courts Act 2003 and Regulation 6 of the High Court Enforcement Officers Regulations 2004.

Under the previous system, the Sheriff was appointed to hold office for no more than one year. Although it was common for successive Sheriffs to appoint the same individuals to the post of Under Sheriff to maintain continuity and experience in the post, there was no compulsion on the Sheriff for him to do so.

The Sheriffs and Under Sheriffs can trace their origins back to Saxon times when they were primarily concerned with the administration of the Shires into which Anglo Saxon England was divided. During the following centuries their powers gradually increased. Unfortunately, this led to corruption and their powers were subsequently limited by various statutes. In the 19th century the offices of Sheriff and Under Sheriff were placed on a more structured footing by the Sheriffs Acts of 1837 and 1887.

Although the name has changed from Under Sheriff to High Court Enforcement Officer there remains a considerable degree of continuity as many of the current HCEOs were previously Under Sheriffs. This has helped to ensure that the expertise and professionalism of the Under Sheriffs continues in the new system.

Procedure

When a creditor issues legal proceedings against another and succeeds in obtaining judgment, the latter becomes the judgment debtor and is consequently liable for the amount awarded against him by the court. Judgment debtors are sometimes 'reluctant' to pay the amount due but the creditor has a number of options at his disposal, one of which is to apply to the High Court to issue a Writ of Execution (known as a 'Writ of Fieri Facias' or 'Writ of Fi Fa'). The Writ is addressed to an Authorized High Court Enforcement Officer and is his authority to 'execute' the Writ by either collecting the money owed under the judgment or by seizing sufficient of the judgment debtor's goods to be sold at auction to raise the funds owed (sometimes referred to as 'satisfying the debt').

Other methods available for obtaining payment of the judgment debt include: obtaining a Charging Order, which secures the judgment debt against the debtor's property; attachment of earnings, which requires an employer of a judgment debtor to make regular deductions from the debtor's earnings towards paying off the debt; and third-party debt orders, where a third party who owes money to the judgment debtor is required to pay it directly to the judgment creditor. Although these other methods of recovering the debt can be effective, they usually take longer to conclude and may be more expensive than enforcement via an HCEO.

High Court Enforcement Officers are 'Officers of the Court' and not agents for the party endeavouring to enforce. The HCEO is responsible for the proper enforcement of the Writ and is answerable to the High Court for the conduct of both himself and his staff during the enforcement process. The consequences of this responsibility cannot be too strongly emphasized. Should the HCEO or any of his staff be found to have committed a serious offence, then not only could he lose his authorization and his livelihood but so also could all of those working for him. For this reason it is important that HCEOs work to a very high standard. This places on them a much higher level of responsibility than other enforcement agents. For example, certificated bailiffs (sometimes referred to as private bailiffs) can have their certificates revoked by the courts, though this would only affect the individual, leaving the firm he worked for free to continue trading. County Court bailiffs (who currently have the sole right to enforce County Court judgments below £600 and judgments regulated under the Consumer Credit Act 1974) are civil servants employed by Her Majesty's Court Service and may be disciplined under civil service procedures.

It has already been mentioned that HCEOs can enforce County Court judgments over £600. In order to do this a judgment creditor needs to 'transfer up' the County Court judgment to the High Court. The procedure is a simple one and most HCEOs will provide a free service to creditors across England and Wales.

The HCEO will always prefer to recover the money owed rather than deprive a judgment debtor of his goods. Nevertheless the power to remove goods is there and the HCEO will use it if necessary. He can only take goods that are owned by the judgment debtor or are jointly owned. If there is a dispute as to the ownership of goods the HCEO can apply to the court, by what is known as an 'interpleader' summons, for it to decide on the ownership.

The HCEO must leave behind sufficient goods to meet the basic domestic needs of the judgment debtor and his or her family as well as any items that constitute the tools of his or her trade. There can often be disagreement over this last point, especially when it involves the possible removal of a motor vehicle. In those circumstances the HCEO may apply to the court for a decision as to whether such goods are necessary for the debtor's work.

In addition to the above there are certain items that HCEOs cannot remove. These include:

■ Items, including cars, office furniture and machinery, that are leased, rented or are on hire purchase agreements;
■ Goods that may have already been seized by any other type of bailiff or enforcement officer.
■ Goods belonging to someone other than the judgment debtor, usually referred to as the 'Third Party'. However, where there is a dispute as to ownership the 'interpleader' process, described above, may be used.

Sometimes a judgment debtor may accept that he or she owes the amount due but is physically incapable of paying the whole of the debt in one go. The HCEO will try to reach agreement with the judgment debtor as to when the sum is to be paid. If the debtor proposes payment by instalments the HCEO will contact the creditor to ask if the proposed instalment terms are acceptable. If they are the HCEO will prepare a list of the judgment debtor's goods that will be sold if the debt is not paid or the debtor fails to meet the instalment payments. The debtor will then be asked to sign a document called a 'Walking Possession Agreement' which lists the items concerned and binds the debtor not to dispose of those goods until payment has been made in full. This arrangement enables the debtor to keep his or her goods and continue to use them provided the payments are made as agreed. If the debtor fails to make the agreed payments the HCEO may then remove the goods and sell them.

Cost of enforcement

One issue of considerable interest to those seeking to enforce their judgments is the cost of such enforcement. In spite of it being the High Court, the costs to the creditor are very reasonable. There is an initial fee of £50 payable to the Court on the issuing of the Writ of Execution. The only other fee the Creditor may have to pay is an abortive fee of £60 plus VAT if the HCEO is unsuccessful in enforcing the Writ. All other fees and charges are payable by the judgment debtor and are recovered by the HCEO as part of the enforcement process.

Enforcement of County Court judgments by County Court bailiffs also incurs fees. Interestingly, following the coming into force of the Civil Proceedings Fees (Amendment) Order 2009, the fees for enforcement in the County Court have been increased to the extent that it is now cheaper for a judgment creditor to transfer his judgment to the High Court for an HCEO to enforce!

Power and responsibility

As stated earlier in this chapter, HCEOs are required to act to the highest standards. Failure to do so may result in loss of livelihood, not only for themselves but also for those who work for them. Although HCEOs have considerable power, including requiring the police to support them in their task of enforcement by ensuring that they are not obstructed in their duties, with such power comes responsibility. HCEOs comply with the provisions of the National Standards for Enforcement Agents published in 2002 by what was then the Lord Chancellor's Department (now the Ministry of Justice). One area of particular concern is that of dealing with vulnerable situations. HCEOs are trained to recognize situations where the debtor is vulnerable and will use his or her discretion as to what action to take, frequently referring back to the creditor to report the circumstances he or she has found. Those recognized as being vulnerable include:

- the elderly;
- people with a disability;
- the seriously ill;
- the recently bereaved;
- single parent families;
- pregnant women;
- unemployed people;
- those whose first language is not English.

The above is not a finite list and HCEOs will assess each situation as it arises.

In the opposite corner, so to speak, from those who can properly be described as vulnerable debtors stand those who are often referred to as the 'won't pays' rather than the 'can't pays'. These are people who are more than capable of meeting any judgment imposed by the courts but simply choose not to do so. The wording on the Writ of Fi Fa commands the HCEO to 'seize and sell' the goods of the debtor.

Although the HCEO has considerable discretion in how he or she interprets that command, if he fails to carry it out to the best of his endeavours he may well find himself being sued by the creditor for failing to meet his obligations. While his actions in dealing with 'vulnerable' people must be measured and appropriate, so should his actions in dealing with the 'won't pays' and the HCEO will make it very clear to such people that if they fail to pay the judgment debt, they may well find their cherished BMW or Range Rover put on the back of a car transporter and taken away for sale. It does not necessarily stop there and in recent times HCEOs have seized and removed aeroplanes!

Additional services

In addition to recovering judgment debts through the use of a Writ of Fi Fa, HCEOs also have the power to recover land after the court has made an order for possession. This is done through the issue of a Writ of Possession. In some circumstances, where a court has ordered recovery of both money and land, a combined Writ of Possession and Fi Fa can be issued.

As well as their main task of recovering money and property under a judgment, HCEOs may also offer creditors other services. In addition to the free service for transferring up County Court judgments to the High Court (see above) they will also arrange for the removal of goods taken into possession during the enforcement process and, if necessary, their subsequent sale. Preparing reports and carrying out tracings and investigations are also some of the services offered.

Furthermore, the enforcing of foreign judgments, particular those from mainland Europe, is becoming an important part of the HCEO's work and is likely to become ever more so in the future. In acknowledging the importance of this work the High Court Enforcement Officers Association, which is the professional, representative organization for HCEOs, has become a member of the Union Internationale des Huissiers de Justice et Officiers Judiciaires (UIHJ), which is the main international body for enforcement officers. This is to ensure that the particular needs and responsibilities of HCEOs in England and Wales are recognized internationally (Scotland and Northern Ireland have their own systems of enforcement). The Association has taken this further by setting up a 'cab rank' system of those of its members who are prepared to take on the work of enforcing foreign judgments.

In recent times, there has been a tendency for mass demonstrations and protests against controversial building projects such as airport runways and new motorways. These protests can take the form of mass occupations of building sites, leading not only to considerable delays and consequential financial penalties to the developers, but also potential danger to those taking part in the protests. A developer will usually apply to the court for an order for their removal. Over the years HCEOs have developed a considerable expertise in dealing with these situations. In more recent times, some protestors have deliberately placed themselves in jeopardy by taking up positions in tree tops or digging extensive underground tunnels as well as sometimes chaining themselves high up on buildings. HCEOs have developed considerable expertise in handling these situations, working with the emergency services to ensure that all Health & Safety requirements are met so as to ensure that not only is the property recovered, but that also the protestors, and those seeking to remove them, remain safe at all times.

Conclusion

High Court Enforcement Officers provide a quality enforcement service to judgment creditors. Although their title is a new one, they come from a long and celebrated tradition of enforcement that can be traced back many centuries. Furthermore they continue to adapt to modern requirements. For example, they have recently been appointed by the Lord Chancellor to be the enforcement officers responsible for recovering awards made by Employment Tribunals. They are highly regulated and, as officers of the court, are answerable to the courts for their behaviour and not to the government or other private sector bodies. In short they provide an efficient, cost-effective and highly responsible service to the public.

Part 4

Customer management

You've spent years building good relationships with your customers...

...why destroy them in an afternoon?

The most common reason for late payment is that your customer has financial problems. Most companies with financial problems recover. Who will those customers deal with when times get better, the supplier who worked with them in the difficult times or the supplier whose first reaction was to resort to legal action and threats?

Contact Resolvent to find out how we'll work with you and your customers in a fresh constructive way to help you collect your debts and build better long term customer relationships.

Resolvent Ltd
- Better collection rates
- Won't alienate your customers
- A more profitable future for you

Resolvent
0800 123 4567

www.resolvent.co.uk

Soft debt collection – collecting money without alienating your customer

Stewart Lund, Resolvent Ltd

It's a classic dilemma – one of your biggest customers has got behind with paying bills, you're given the usual excuses but still payment isn't forthcoming. With a smaller debt you'd probably commence your normal debt collection process – a letter from a solicitor or debt collection company, possibly followed by action in the County Court – however, once you start down this road you're likely to ruin your relationship with an important customer permanently.

Naturally, you can't ignore the late payment because if the customer is in trouble it's vital not to be the last one in the queue, but, equally, pushing too hard when they might only have short-term cash-flow problems could lose a customer in whom you've invested a lot of time and money in acquisition and development. Pushing too hard can also tip a customer over the edge into insolvency, in which case you may receive nothing, whereas understanding their problems (and where appropriate being flexible) may put you in a much better position. The key word here is 'understanding', as we shall see.

'Speak softly and carry a big stick'

These wise words spoken by Theodore Roosevelt in 1901 reflect the underlying ethos of soft debt collection. Soft Debt Collection (SDC) is not a soft option, simply a softer approach, with the understanding between the parties that if the debtor doesn't accept the outstretched hand, then a more formal debt collection process is bound to follow. SDC is the process of understanding your customer's business and their reasons for not paying, and choosing the appropriate course of action. Though legal action is rarely the most effective solution, the implicit knowledge that it is available as a last resort serves to ensure that the debtor gives SDC their full attention.

How soft debt collection affects customer relationships

The first thing to remember always is that your customer is in business too, just like you are, and they'll be fully aware that you need to collect your debts in order to keep your own business running. During the life cycle of most SME businesses there will be periods when cash flow is tight. SDC is about appointing an experienced firm to work with your customer and to understand the issues that they're facing. The solution for collecting debts will be different depending on what's happening within your customer's business; so, for example, it is important to understand whether it is a short-term matter or whether the business is in terminal decline, and to work out a way of supporting them through this period.

Traditional debt collection models are a blunt instrument and they do not take the time to understand your customer and their issues, adopting a 'one size fits all' approach that may or may not be appropriate. One thing is certain – a customer who has been treated with understanding will remember which suppliers did this when times were difficult and which suppliers took a more aggressive approach.

Surely I can do this on my own?

Although you will probably discuss some matters with your customers, and there may be very good personal relationships that have built up over the years between you, there are many benefits to using a third-party specialist to work with you. By using a specialist professional firm you first communicate the message to your customer that the matter is serious, but by having not gone down a traditional debt collection route with all the antagonism that this involves you've not put your customer into a corner where they'll behave defensively.

A firm experienced in SDC will know how to approach your customer and present their role as someone who is going to be able to help them to resolve the problems they're probably experiencing rather than add to them. Your customer will also generally be far more ready to open up about their business when talking to an independent professional advisor, and this deeper understanding of their business issues is likely to lead to a far more appropriate solution being found.

Choosing a representative

Selecting the best firm or individual to represent you is vital to a successful outcome when using SDC. An approach from a traditional debt collection agency will immediately put your customer on the defensive. Using a solicitor may be better, but few are experienced with this style of working, preferring a more formulaic approach to debt collection. A firm that specializes in SDC will be experienced at reading between the lines of what is said to them and identifying the real underlying issues with your customer. Their experience of dealing with businesses in difficulty will give them both a far better understanding of the problems that businesses go through, how to manage those problems and also a wide range of solutions that are tried and tested. A specialist will also be fully conversant with the full range of legal options available to them if the softer approach fails.

Finally, using a firm that has a detailed knowledge of debt collection, legal action and the insolvency laws will ensure that the correct solution is always applied as early as possible and give a far better chance of collecting your debt.

Process

The process in SDC is all-important and we shall consider here the various steps that will be undertaken by a firm specializing in SDC.

Introduction to the debtor

The introduction to the debtor, and the way this is done, is vital to building a working relationship with them. Introductions will be made at a senior level to ensure that the right people are involved in the process. Even more importantly, it will be explained to the debtor that this is an alternative to a more aggressive form of debt collection because you want to work constructively with your customer rather than create more problems for them.

Reconciling ledgers

The most common reasons for non-payment of invoices and debts are disputes, or that your customer doesn't agree with your statement and hasn't spent the time to reconcile it. Ensuring that both you and your customer agree on what is payable is essential and where genuine disputes exist the firm you use can often act as mediator to resolve these issues too.

Understanding your customer

The most fundamental part of SDC is understanding your customer and their business. If the matter has already reached a point where you've felt the need to retain a firm to collect the debt, then the chances are that your customer has cash-flow problems.

Finding the solution

From the understanding gained in the earlier steps a plan of action can be agreed that meets both the supplier's and customer's needs. The bottom line will be that the debt must be paid, but there are a very wide range of ways in which this can be done and scheduled, and tools to ensure that the debt is secured where appropriate. The solution will be designed to allow the trading relationship to be maintained in both the short and long term, the supplier to have their debt paid and an enhanced relationship between the two.

Future dealings

Collecting debts in the traditional manner of solicitor's letters and legal action will produce results in some circumstances but one inevitable consequence will be the loss of your customer. Of course, a customer who doesn't pay their bills is probably not a customer that you want to keep, but more often than not there will be short-term cash-flow issues that lie behind those late payments and there exist opportunities to generate future profits from that customer. It is an old adage that it costs far more to win a new customer than keep an existing one and that underlying truth shapes every step of the process with SDC. It is invariably the case in situations where SDC has been used to collect debts, that far from the supplier–customer relationship being damaged, it is enhanced. The understanding and support that is given by the supplier, though done for their own ends of collecting the debt, is seen by the customer as a form of support, which differentiates that supplier from the others with which they deal. It's common for trade between the two to increase after the debt issues have been resolved rather than fall as it would with more traditional methods of debt collection.

Soft debt collection in practice

Resolvent are specialists in soft debt collection and our experience ensures that we have one of the best collection rates in the industry. Whereas other approaches to debt collection can be impersonal and aggressive, experience tells us that SDC works best when carried out face to face. When tackling an assignment we always insist on meeting with the debtor in person for a number of reasons:

- it usually means that we can discuss matters with a decision maker rather than a more junior member of staff;
- people find it much more difficult not to be honest about payment when you're talking to them face to face;
- by building a relationship with individuals it is generally easier to resolve any issues that might develop in the future.

Below is a practical example of a client who came to us with a typical problem of not wishing to take legal action against their customer but also needing the certainty that they were going to be paid for their work.

Case Study

Company ABC Ltd provides specialist metal engineering services to a range of clients from local construction firms to major blue-chip food processing companies. ABC turns over approximately £4.5 million and among this were a few customers each representing over 10 per cent of total turnover and whose custom was highly profitable to ABC. One of these customers, XYZ Ltd, had always paid on time, but in late 2008 ABC was having to chase for every payment and payments were consistently arriving outside their due dates. This situation worsened and despite regular calls from the credit controller at ABC, and even calls from the directors of ABC, the situation still did not improve. The directors of ABC felt they were being given excuses about why payment could not be made on time that they simply did not believe. Eventually a debt of almost £200,000 had built up that wasn't being reduced and ABC were acutely aware that the consequence of this amount becoming bad would probably be their own insolvency.

In January 2009, the directors of ABC contacted their accountant for advice and their accountant put them in touch with Resolvent whose approach is deliberately non-confrontational and differs markedly from the usual threats made by debt collection agencies to recover monies owed. Instead of sending a letter out of the blue, we asked the directors of ABC who already had a personal relationship with XYZ to call their customer and introduce us. In this way we were sure that we would be talking to the decision makers at XYZ.

We then arranged to meet with XYZ and explained that ABC valued their custom and had no desire to go down the usual debt collection route with them but, of course, could not let the debt build up because of the knock-on impact on their cash flow. Invariably, we find that because we are a third party and have not been part of the often fractious interaction in the build-up to the outstanding debt, the debtor company is willing to be far more open and candid with us; and this was indeed the case here.

Our first task was to work through the outstanding invoices one by one, to ensure that the two companies agreed on what invoices had been sent and what had been paid – this removes one potential reason for not paying. We resolved nearly 20 differences on ledgers where invoices had been missed or payments mis-posted.

Our second task was to isolate any disputed invoices and agree that all the remainder were due and payable. We then worked through the disputed ones, resolving any problems by ensuring delivery notes and other supporting documents could be produced where required and also mediated on two invoices where there were issues of late supply and quality issues. At the end of this process both companies agreed exactly on the outstanding balance.

Next we tried to agree a payment schedule with XYZ but found they were unwilling to commit to firm dates. As part of our negotiations we explained that our role was to avoid any legal action but if we couldn't reach agreement with them we would have no choice but to recommend to ABC that they commenced legal action. As the debt was not disputed (we had been though this earlier with them) this could take the form of County Court action, or even a winding-up petition. Further discussions ensued, always amicable and professional. We were even shown copies of XYZ's management accounts and business plan and it soon became clear that the reason for the late payments was that the sale of a freehold building that they owned had been delayed far longer than they had expected, depriving the company of cash that they had relied on receiving. Once we fully understood the problem we were able to agree with XYZ that their solicitor would give ABC an undertaking that their debt would be paid from the sale proceeds of the building, thus giving ABC the security of knowing their debt was to be paid, and also giving them the comfort to carry on trading with XYZ while the matter was resolved. ABC found that their understanding and reluctance to follow conventional debt collection routes was further rewarded by an enhanced relationship with their customer and a significant increase in the volume of trade between the two.

Summary

Soft debt collection isn't the best solution for every problem. Small debts are better collected through more traditional means because of the amount of time required, but for larger debts, and where the value of keeping the customer is high, it is invariably worth the investment.

Rewarding.

Protect your company from bad debt and help it grow

In today's economic climate, whether your company is an SME, UK corporate or a multinational, can you afford to ignore credit risk?

At Aon Trade Credit, whatever your company's business — from jewellery manufacturing to seafood distribution — we work with you to find the best solution to **protect your business** against bad debt and reinforce your **credit management** processes. This could help you to **reap the reward** of expanding into new or uncertain markets.

And of course as the **UK's leading broker***, we're used to helping with credit risk management which can give access to additional finance if you need it.

Contact Amy Slayford on **020 7882 0146** or email atc@aon.co.uk

Customer insight – knowing your customer to help reduce your credit risk

Amy Slayford, Aon Trade Credit

Introduction

There is no need to further emphasize the impact of the credit crunch on the UK economy. The figures speak for themselves. Business insolvencies in England and Wales rose by 24 per cent in 2008 compared to 2007 (see Figure 4.2.1) and figures from the first quarter of 2009 show a massive increase of 57 per cent from the same period the previous year (see Figure 4.2.2). How certain are you that one of your customers won't be next? Following some of the advice and the steps contained in this article won't halt their demise, but it might help you reduce your credit risk exposure.

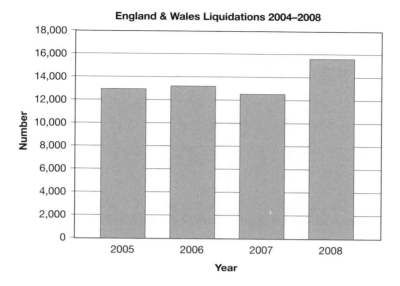

Figure 4.2.1 England and Wales Liquidations 2004–08
Source: Department of National Statistics (UK Govt)

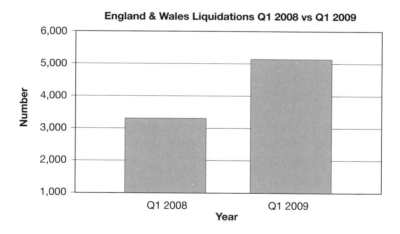

Figure 4.2.2 England and Wales Liquidations Q1 2008 vs Q1 2009
Source: Department of National Statistics (UK Govt)

Know your customer

In today's environment, customer transparency is paramount. Although it may seem that information on your customers is hard to come by, there are several steps that you can take to protect your balance sheet without necessarily incurring any additional costs.

Pre-sale with existing or new customers

Perform a credit check with a trustworthy source

There are a number of reputable credit reference agencies within the UK market offering reports containing financial and management information on most companies around the world. Some countries are more difficult to attain information on as they may not have a legal requirement to file their accounts, but essentially this is a good place to start. Key information providers include Dun & Bradstreet, Equifax, Experian and Graydon, though there are others available. These reports will give you an indication of the status agency's overall credit risk assessment of the company along with more detailed information such as a financial summary and a list of the key executives.

You should not, however, treat credit reference information as the be all and end all – they give their opinion based on information they have access to and your personal experience with a customer might be entirely different. The key is to take a balanced view. Remember to keep updating your business information reports – a report from two years ago will not be worth the paper it's written on.

Meet your client

This may sound obvious, but a large proportion of business now is conducted over the phone or via the internet, so it can be difficult to gain a meaningful impression of who you are dealing with. Wherever possible when looking to begin a new business relationship – go and meet them. Seeing their business in operation can give you a greater understanding of how they run the company and provide a level of intuition only achievable in the flesh.

Check their family tree

Who is their parent company? Are they part of a large group with a strong brand and financial status or is their parent constantly in the headlines as under threat of collapse? These factors can have an impact on their respective financial standing. You should also consider external market conditions, eg impact of economic decline on the manufacturing or automotive industries. How might this affect your (prospective) customer?

Where are they based?

If they are based in the United Kingdom, it is fairly safe to assume it improbable they will suffer from an interruption in their business due, for example, to a political embargo. If they are based in a non-OECD country, however, you will need to consider any external factors that might affect their ability to pay and take steps accordingly. Such issues could include war, political sanctions, introduction of despotic regimes or restricted access to foreign exchange. Belgian export credit agency Ducroire Delcredere offers a complimentary country risk information service on their website that is often useful for country updates.

Who do they bank with?

This may be difficult information to obtain, but it's more possible that if they bank with a recognized or high-street name the lending criteria used is of a decent level of stringency. The availability of credit extended to them should, in principle, reflect their liquidity and the quality of their internal credit management procedures.

Where else is their finance coming from?

Do a little digging and investigate the company's ownership. Look at who its investors are and if possible their motivation. Do they have to consider shareholders' interests? If they are part of a group, what are the other subsidiaries doing? These factors will help build a strategic profile of the company – eg are they interested in making a quick buck or in fulfilling long-term objectives?

Who are they supplying?

If you sell a product, research and assess the end-user/recipient. Market trends dictate fluctuations in supply and demand and if your potential customer is supplying to a sector in decline you will need to take their future ability to distribute the product into consideration.

Contract with the correct entity

You must have the correct legal entity of the company you are trading with. This is essential if you have credit insurance, as in the event of a claim you will not be covered if you have the wrong principal to contract. Ask for their company registration number and check it online with Companies House, or your country's domestic equivalent, before agreeing terms.

Each customer will be different and only you have a true knowledge of how your business runs; however, the above steps can help you assess your overall credit risk with a company and set reasonable credit terms for your customers while remaining commercially minded.

Post-sale and supplying existing customers

Unfortunately, the hard work does not end once you have set your credit terms. You will need to ensure that you continue to monitor your portfolio of customers by reassessing the overall risk on a regular basis. The following steps can help you do this and, as expected, support good credit management principles.

Maintain a dialogue with your customer

Once you have established a good rapport with your client, it would be a shame to waste it. Continue to speak to them and, if possible, visit them to gain insight into how their business is performing. Simple things like seeing what their stock levels are like on site can help you get a picture of their financial state.

Keep your credit checks up to date

As mentioned above, it is essential to update your credit reference information. Whatever means you use, it is so important to have current (or as near to) financial information on your customers. As we have witnessed in the UK since mid-2008 and throughout 2009, even well-established companies can decline with frightening velocity.

Monitor payment behaviour

As we know, good credit management is fundamental to any successful business. Once you are trading with your customer you need to carefully monitor their activities – especially when it comes to payment delinquency. If you use credit insurance, you will need to report overdue invoices according to the terms and conditions of your policy, but overdue reporting is good practice in any event. Other signs to look for are sudden requests for changes to terms or means of payment.

Monitor managerial or structural changes to the business

Have you dealt with three different Financial Controllers in as many months? Have they rebranded their company recently after a major buyout? Changes to a company's structure or management may imply they intend to change their business strategy or that they are experiencing financial difficulties. Watch out for mergers and acquisitions and high staff turnover, and if really concerned, track information in the press.

Join a credit circle

There's nothing quite like gaining information from your peers. Sharing experiences and knowledge is invaluable and although there are clear rules around the level of information that can be shared in such forums, it can give you a greater understanding of any issues in your sector of which you may as yet be unaware. Such events are also great for networking – meaning you may well find opportunities for new business.

Follow market trends

Whatever your sector, keeping abreast of news and trends is crucial to maintaining a profitable business and expanding sales. Use whatever resources you have to make sure you are up to date with news and innovative ideas in your industry. This will help you to forecast future developments in your sector – both positive and negative.

Although the above may seem terribly ominous, it is not all doom and gloom! Good credit management and careful monitoring of payment trends, etc can only help you grow your business. Sales and credit control can work together and if you take some or all of the steps above this will only deepen your customer insight, giving opportunities for new business and increased sales with existing customers.

Solutions to help you manage credit risk

Although sound credit management practices are vital, there will always be scenarios that you simply cannot predict. The following solutions can help you manage your credit risk and enhance cash flow during those times.

Credit insurance

Credit insurance protects you from the impact of bad debt, whether through insolvency or non-payment, by insuring your credit risk. It is available for companies of all sizes and sectors and premium is quoted based on a full credit risk assessment of your individual business. The key benefit of credit insurance, apart from balance sheet protection, is customer insight. Underwriters hold an extensive library of information, the majority of which is outside of the public domain. As they are the ones taking on the risk, it is in their interest to have deep buyer knowledge and they gain this from buyer visits, overdue payment information submitted by clients and in-house economic and sector analysis. The insured credit limit levels they set on your customers are based on this stringent risk assessment and can give you protection on your balance sheet when you need it most. It is worth mentioning that the disciplines needed to run a credit insurance policy are supported by good credit management and they work very much hand in hand.

Credit management consultancy

The use of a credit management audit can be invaluable. Familiarity can easily slip into complacency, and there are genuine benefits in having an expert with an unbiased eye assess your credit management processes.

Business information

As mentioned above, business and status information is available in a number of different guises. You can choose the format that suits both your business and your budget. For example, Aon's online business information platform, Aon Trade Link, offers reports from the aforementioned key providers on a 'pay-as-you-use' basis; visit www.aon.co.uk/tradelink.

Credit risk diagnostic tools

Credit risk diagnostic tools such as Aon Trade Manager (ATM) can help you gain a true picture of your customers' payment trends and your total credit risk exposure. ATM takes daily feeds directly from your accounts receivables system and analyses payment data to give you a weekly recommended credit limit on each of your customers. If your trading experience is insufficient, or you want a second opinion, you can also append status agency information to attain a blended limit on your overall credit risk. This allows you to spot customers demonstrating delinquent payment behaviour more quickly and highlights those that consistently pay on or before terms so you can follow up with a sales call. For more information on ATM, visit www.aontrademanager.com.

Trade finance

Trade finance funds the gap between the purchase and sale of a product or service. It can be facilitated in many ways, but its fundamental aim is to enable companies to use their receivables asset to reduce cash-flow pressure and in some cases give access to additional lines of finance. Trade finance banks are more likely to lend on better and more flexible terms when there is a credit insurance policy in place as this acts as security against its liability. Trade finance can give access to additional working capital, on cheaper and more flexible terms, and can complement your existing banking relationships.

Consider using a trade credit broker

Using a trade credit broker brings a wealth of benefits, such as innovative product knowledge, unbiased advice and intermediary support, when liaising with credit insurers or banks for trade finance. They can offer you objective guidance in all areas of trade receivable management and technical expertise in the design and placement of your chosen trade credit solution. Managing a credit insurance policy is a 'hands-on' business and your specialist broker can give you ongoing policy management support, particularly valuable in the event of a claim.

Conclusion

In our current economic times, credit management within a business is an unenviable task. There can never be 100 per cent certainty to each decision you take, but with careful planning, investigation and monitoring it is possible to control your credit risk. Heightening your customer awareness will result in a deepening of your customer insight, allowing you to trade with a degree of certainty in an uncertain world.

With over 42 years of publishing, more than 80 million people have succeeded in business with thanks to **Kogan Page**

www.koganpage.com

You are reading one of the thousands of books published by **Kogan Page**. As Europe's leading independent business book publishers **Kogan Page** has always sought to provide up-to-the-minute books that offer practical guidance at affordable prices.

KoganPage

Debt collection – the right attitude

Zoe Lacey, Mint Credit Management UK Ltd

Introduction

Effective control of cash flow is vital to the operational success of any business, particularly during periods of economic downturn. A proactive approach to credit management and debt recovery is imperative in ensuring that debt collection does not become a costly and time-intensive activity.

Increasing UK personal debt and a rise in the number of administrations and insolvencies, including bankruptcy, has affected both consumer and commercial collections. Macro-economic conditions have severely impacted the collectability of accounts, unemployment being the highest ranked economic factor.

Recent changes in the economy as a result of the financial crisis have put pressure on the marketplace and companies, large and small, to expand collections functions and implement strategies to reduce delinquency, maximize collections performance and increase cash flow. This growing pressure coupled with evolving legislation and regulation of the industry means that companies are being forced to increase their resources to enhance collections capability and focus their attention on certain elements of the collections cycle. The implementation of the Consumer Credit Act 2006 increased consumer protection; intense media attention and data quality issues are just some of the driving forces.

Pre-delinquency management

Pre-delinquency management is widely used internally by companies, particularly by financial institutions to identify early trigger signs that customers may be falling into financial difficulty. The impact of a pre-emptive or responsive strategy is highly effective in preventing customers defaulting or making late payments. Internal data may be adverse and identify the customer as over-indebted or external data from a credit reference bureau may provide an alert notification that another creditor has taken action against your customer. The causes of over-indebtedness may include changes in customer circumstances or behaviour due to unforeseen life events such as ill health, unemployment, etc. Appropriate action can be taken by the creditor accordingly to raise the customer's awareness or provide assistance in dealing with debt.

When an overdue account reaches the end of the in-house collections cycle, and it is apparent that the debtor is delaying payment or refusing to pay, a company may choose to continue to work the account, write it off, outsource and place it with a debt collection agency or sell the debt.

Outsourcing solutions

Outsourcing debts can be a short-term option to ease excess inventory or a long-term option to reduce the cost of in-house collection and can easily be scaled up and down depending on volume.

Organizations are increasingly recognizing that utilizing the services of a Debt Collection Agency (DCA) should be an integral part of a company's credit management strategy. DCAs offer third-party intervention when in-house efforts have been exhausted. Some customers ignore reminders and wait until they receive a significant warning, often the threat of legal action. Working in partnership with a debt collection agency to outsource collections provides many benefits. Debts can be outsourced at various stages of the collection cycle, from the early stage of collection through to write-off.

Outsourcing to an agency strengthens the collections process in showing debtors that the creditor is serious about taking further action to recover monies owed to them. Agencies have specialist knowledge of the skills required to collect debt, including a good understanding of the legal procedures, and are able to commit more time to collecting your money. Most importantly, agencies will be familiar with the minefield of legislation and regulation governing their business activities and most will have a dedicated compliance officer to ensure that their practices and procedures remain fully compliant. Outsourcing also releases valuable resource to allow a company's in-house collections team to remain focused on large, currently active accounts where they are able to achieve maximum recovery. Most agencies work on a no-recovery no-fee basis, with a percentage commission being levied on any amount recovered. The fee charged will depend on the complexity and volume. Depending on the type of debt, 80 per cent of debt can be collected within 30 days because of the 'third-party effect' and full-time resources applied.

In selecting the right agency, a company will consider an amalgamation of factors including ensuring that the agency has the necessary trading licences and registrations, experience and skill sets to do the job in accordance with legislation and regulatory guidelines. The majority of reputable agencies are members of the Credit Services Association (CSA). The CSA is the only national association in the UK for business in the credit support sectors, such as debt collection, status enquires and tracing, debt outsourcing, debt purchase and other allied activities.

Members of the CSA are bound by the CSA Code of Practice and are actively involved in promoting best practice within the credit industry. DCAs are also required to comply with the OFT Debt Collection Guidance. Clients are therefore assured that strict codes of conduct are adhered to at all times during their business activities in order to set higher standards of best practice, ethics and fairness in dealing with your customers.

Members of the CSA are responsible for an estimated 95 per cent of all debt collection activity undertaken by creditors through external debt collection agencies. The total volume of debt handled by CSA members on a contingency basis reaches in excess of £15 billion per annum. This represents more than 20 million individual debt cases.[1]

The approach of a debt collection agency (DCA)

At Mint Credit Management UK Ltd (MCM), highly trained collectors use a combination of collection methodologies and sophisticated techniques to achieve quick and efficient recovery of debts according to client requirements. A 'one size fits all' approach, treating all accounts the same over a period of time, is no longer effective. Identifying segments with different behaviour and tailoring activity accordingly will achieve better results, maximizing recovery and ultimately net profit.

By implementing a customer-centric approach to debt recovery, creditors and debt collection agencies are able to develop successful customer contact and engagement strategies. Collectors are trained to use their negotiation skills to engage with the debtor as opposed to confronting them, a firm but fair approach that maintains the creditor and debtor relationship where possible and is successful in rehabilitating customers. Each and every case is assessed on its own merits and collectors adopt an effective collection strategy to suit the circumstances of the debtor. During the process, collectors gather as much information about the debtor as possible in order to assess their ability and willingness to settle what is owed.

Litigation

Despite best efforts, it is inevitable that legal proceedings will sometimes be necessary, particularly where a debt is disputed. However, non-court action can also be an effective tool in resolving disputes. Provided both parties agree, such options include negotiation, mediation, conciliation or arbitration and their use is encouraged by the Courts to facilitate early settlement and reduce the caseload on the Court system.

Prior to issuing legal proceedings it is good practice to check the credit worthiness of your customer to ensure they have the means to settle. Pre-sue reports will determine the viability of legal action and whether it is cost effective to pursue. Having identified the current financial circumstances of the individual or business, this information can be used to determine the most suitable method of enforcement should you be successful in obtaining judgment.

For commercial debts, an effective tool in negotiating settlement is the application of late payment legislation. The Late Payment of Commercial Debts (Interest) Act 1998 was introduced by UK Government to provide businesses with a statutory right to claim interest and reasonable debt recovery costs from other businesses for the late payment of commercial debt. Implementation of the Act was designed to help promote a prompt payment culture. The right to exercise your statutory right and apply it will depend on existing terms and conditions of the business in relation to debt recovery. The interest rate a business can charge is set twice annually on 30 June and 31 December using the Bank of England base rate as the reference rate, plus eight per cent. The legislation sets out a schedule of reasonable debt recovery costs that can be charged to late-paying customers. The costs are £40 for debts under £1,000, £70 for debts between £1,000 and £10,000 and £100 for debts over £10,000.[2]

Case Study 1 – Commercial recovery

A leading developer and provider of industry-specific software applications and business solutions, our client employs around 250 people operating from business offices in the United Kingdom and Ireland.

On completing an internal review of their third-party debt collection agent, our client decided to terminate the existing contract based on a number of factors. In terms of performance and collections success, it was felt that the agency did not have the level of experience and technology required to improve on its current collection success rate. The agent was not providing a timely high standard of account management information and customer service. A lack of investment also meant the agent did not have adequate reporting tools, for example, client online reporting.

Our client considered creating their own in-house collections team, but a management review identified that the time and resources required would detract from the core business.

Without a dedicated debt recovery process in-house, it was imperative that during the agent selection process they choose an agency with the specialist background required not only to achieve a higher success rate but also to ensure that there would be excellent ongoing customer and account management service.

Subject to a tender process, Mint Credit Management UK Ltd was selected as the preferred agent to provide debt collection services, including trace and investigation and litigation via their nominated solicitors.

The collections software utilized by MCM has been specifically designed and chosen to better serve clients by providing 'snapshot information' at the click of a button through a secure online log-in. The software provides case management and client-specific automated workflows with integrated payment processing. The online client-reporting facility is interactive and allows clients to view the status of accounts daily and load new instructions at their convenience. The client and collectors are able to add notes to individual debt accounts and send messages. Each new instruction is assigned to a member of a dedicated team and all actions diarized to ensure that files are driven towards early settlement by appearing in each team members daily work list.

MCM proposed a bespoke solution, utilizing a comprehensive suite of collection methodologies and in-house collection technology. This ensured that MCM could deliver a high-percentage success rate for this client while also providing a high-standard level of service. The client was able to monitor and check the status of their instructions online 24/7 : 365 and maintain a degree of control over their outsourced debt portfolio.

Case Study 2 – Consumer recovery

MCM were approached by a client to collect outstanding high-value unsecured consumer debts.

Working with the client, a bespoke solution was developed combining a letter suite and contact strategy to engage with the debtors. Initial data provided by the client was automatically processed, cleansed and filtered through multiple sources to obtain new information and enable segmentation. A number of accounts identified potential 'gone aways', and successful trace results located the debtors to a new address where contact could be made. During the process we also identified a certain percentage of home ownership.

MCM worked the accounts using the client-specific workflow system, applying different treatments depending on the debtor's circumstances to achieve successful recovery. Where an amicable settlement was not achievable litigation was commenced and enforcement action taken accordingly to recover the amount owed including legal fees and Court costs. A proportion of debts have also been secured by obtaining a charging order.

Summary

Using the services of a DCA will accelerate your debt recovery processes to save time, money and resources by:

- improving the efficiency of your recovery process and services;
- freeing up valuable administration/credit control resources to focus on more profitable activities;
- ensuring that you maintain and improve company collection success rate;
- providing a level of specialist expertise in debt collection.

Times have changed and consequently collection strategies have also evolved. Strategies for collection are now being built on principles of fairness, transparency and sustainability with the customer at the centre. Legislation and regulations governing the industry continue to be improved to ensure those companies operating in the industry implement policies and procedures to ensure compliance. Drawing on recent experience, creditors and debtors need to take shared responsibility to ensure that there is a balance between responsible lending and responsible borrowing.

Notes

1   Debt Manifesto, The Credit Services Association (CSA).
2   The Late Payment of Commercial Debts Regulations 2002, Statutory Instrument 2002 No. 1674.

Debt recovery and litigation strategies in recessionary times

Trevor Philips, Lovetts

The problem

The current recession has exacerbated many long-term credit and debt recovery issues connected with the basic necessity for businesses to get paid on time. Combine this with the need to brush up on 'front-end' procedures to limit exposure to the type of clients who might fail without warning, leaving large amounts outstanding to their creditors, and you have a potentially toxic cocktail consisting of countless problems for businesses in the United Kingdom (and beyond).

Credit Managers are being faced with an increasingly difficult task of attempting to unearth reliable and up-to-date credit information on prospective and existing clients. An alarming increase in the number of companies going into administration threatens the cash flow of larger businesses and the very survival of smaller businesses, who find out that a client who owes thousands of pounds is no longer trading, leaving them with few options to remedy the situation.

Even among established clients, attempted declarations of unilateral changes to business and payment terms have recently risen to epidemic proportions and, with no quick end in sight to the recession, look set to continue. Businesses are conserving cash by paying suppliers late, not at all or are making partial payment in the belief that the recipient will not make a claim for the remainder due to it being perceived as an uneconomic option. For many smaller companies this can spell disaster for their attempts to survive in a very difficult financial situation, and for larger entities the cash-flow implications can rapidly move beyond it being just a nuisance. On a macro-economic level the whole issue of debtor attempting to 'move the goal posts' on business and payment terms puts pressure on suppliers, who, in turn, put pressure on their suppliers and so on down the whole chain of supply and demand and beyond.

Despite the current wider economic problems, which appear beyond the control of individual companies, well over 80 per cent of Letters before Action (LBAs) issued by Lovetts on behalf of their client base, are not proceeding any further than that stage. This is despite a considerable rise in the number of LBAs being requested by creditors and the subsequent rise in the number of claims also being sent. The question of why there has not been a more dramatic decline in the effectiveness of LBAs, given the obvious reluctance of debtors to pay what is due when it is due, remains open to discussion.

Does the debtor have a valid dispute?

Before proceeding with using the full powers of recovery you have to hand, it is worth standing back and actually reviewing whether the customer who has not made a payment or is paying late on a regular basis has an actual dispute or has made any complaints to other members of staff of which you may not be aware. Slow or begrudging payments can often be a sign that an established client is not happy with the service they are getting and are not getting the message through via the usual channels. Speak to the relevant line manager, credit controller and other contacts to see if anyone has had direct contact with the debtor in recent days. Even hearsay information can often lead to the root cause of the problem. Picking up the telephone yourself is always a good option as it will clarify the situation pretty swiftly and will be appreciated by a frustrated client.

If there is a valid dispute, make sure all the personnel in your business involved with credit control are aware that there is a dispute, it is being dealt with and that further action is placed on hold to avoid making a bad situation worse.

If there is no valid dispute, then the answer may lie in that there is a 'can pay, just don't want to pay' attitude among many debtors, rather than the perception currently held that those sitting firmly on their money are actually operating in a 'can't pay, won't pay' world. Many businesses just require a well-considered incentive to start regarding the debt owed to *your* business as the one that needs to be settled in priority to other debts that may be residing on their books.

Understanding what you can do as a business to find the edge over other creditors to get paid first can make the difference between success or joining the list of failed companies that did not take control of their ledger properly. So, saying all that, the question remains over how to become an irresistible force when collecting what is due to you.

Give yourself priority status

The most important factor to achieve success is to ensure that it is more expensive and difficult for your debtor to delay paying you than their other creditors. If you are a Financial Director under pressure, the first thing you would attempt to identify when faced with a pile of threatening letters and phone calls, is which creditor is likely to do the most damage to your bank balance, or even threaten your continued existence, if you fail to pay them quickly. Your business can achieve priority status in several ways.

1. Do not be afraid to utilize a solicitor's LBA rapidly if all internally generated correspondence and calls have failed to illicit the required response from the debtor. An LBA implies:

- forthcoming court proceedings; and
- costs being added to the debt which could dramatically raise the sum eventually payable.

Even though most businesses produce letters that are similar in content to a solicitor's LBA, the hard cold truth of the matter is that an LBA received from a solicitor is much more likely to generate a payment or response than an equivalent seven-day letter sent from the credit control section of your average business. The cost of sending an LBA from a solicitor is tiny compared to the impact it generates when received. Not taking advantage of this option does not make sense. Though an LBA is a useful recovery tool, its effectiveness can be diluted if your clients see it used too frequently as part of your day-to-day credit control procedures and start to believe that there is unlikely to be a follow-up. Having blasé debtors who regard your threats as unlikely to be enforced, is not a situation any business wants to be left dealing with when cash flow is vital.

2. Late Payment legislation is under-utilized by many businesses in this country, and can be a highly effective tool in the debt recovery armoury if used correctly. The legislation is clear and easy to use and although it may only be an option if your Terms of Business have no interest provision or expressly include it, if your business can take advantage of the legislation don't hesitate to apply it. Applicable interest rates at eight per cent over Bank of England Base Rate (at the previous 31 December or 30 June) and a minimum charge of £40 per invoice, all helps to make not paying your business an expensive luxury.

To use this legislation you will need to spell out your full claim for costs, interest and compensation in your first letter to the debtor and the Late Payment legislation may well be your best bet, but if the legislation is available, then don't hesitate to apply it as at the end of the day that is what it is there for.

3. Avoid putting off taking action when a debtor is obviously attempting to either delay payment for an unacceptable period of time or appears to have no intention of making a payment at all. If you believe you have exhausted your internal collection procedures, instruct debt recovery lawyers sooner rather than later instead of hanging on forlornly waiting for a cheque to drop though the letter box. Lovetts' latest statistics show that in the month of February 2009 companies were deciding to take the legal route a staggering 39 days sooner than a year previously, and were acting nine days quicker to issue a Claim after LBA in the past quarter than in the same quarter a year ago. These may look like meaningless statistics on an individual company basis but they are actually clear signs which demonstrate that if you decide to delay taking decisive action the debtor will consider you as weak and therefore a low-priority creditor and place you firmly at the back of the queue for payment!

Figure 4.4.1 illustrates the steps in sequential order of effective claim procedure.

How to get quicker resolution:

1. Summary judgment – Reliable and up-to-date legal advice from a reputable solicitor will include advice on potential costs and whether summary judgment is a prospect. As with many things in debt recovery, what options are open to you is based on the quality of the paperwork supporting your claim, and summary judgment is no different in this regard. Litigation that is worthwhile, from a creditor's point of view, is litigation with a real prospect of achieving summary judgment to bring the matter to a swift conclusion.

2. Settlement – As a business you need to decide at the outset what you are prepared to accept as a minimum settlement and what your ultimate aim is from the whole procedure. If summary judgment proves to be a real prospect, then an outright win may well be a possibility. If an outright win is not a possibility, then a quick settlement may be the better option to avoid a lengthy period of litigation and enforcement. Given the lack of time to review what is being offered and the pressurized environment, the worst possible scenario is negotiating a settlement and being forced into acceptance at the door of the Court.

3. Part 36 offers work by putting the opponent at risk of dire costs consequences, ie an order that the party should pay more of your costs than usual with interest on both the costs and the award at a penal rate. This can work as a motivating tool in the right circumstances.

4. Mediation – This involves a third party becoming involved to get the parties talking to each other, understanding each other's position and kick-starting the process of negotiation. A mediated settlement may not be 100 per cent satisfying – indeed it will almost certainly not be – but most mediated settlements do get paid and managements can then get back to running their businesses without being sidetracked on litigation with its attendant costs. Mediation is not for everyone or for every situation but it is a useful option in certain circumstances.

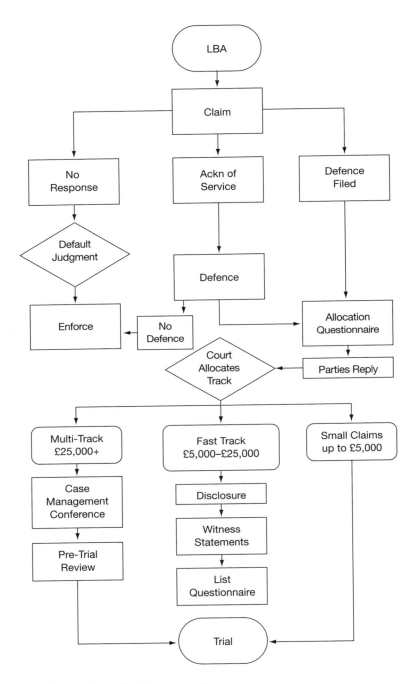

Figure 4.4.1 Flow chart of claim procedure

Avoid wasting money

Get someone senior to intervene

First, nominate a senior person within your organization to be responsible for vetting potential litigation to assess whether the case is really good value for money and even if there is a real dispute driving the process. Misunderstandings can occasionally snowball into a dispute where an earlier meeting to discuss the matter could have potentially avoided the present situation.

Other questions that should be asked are: is there is a potential counterclaim that could arise from taking legal action? Is there a personality clash driving the dispute – one of 'our people' conducting a vendetta with one of 'their people' that has accelerated out of control and is no longer based on the 'facts' of the matter which sparked the dispute? It is surprising how often this happens, particularly when a culture of 'empire building' has established itself within departments. Is it possible that a quiet word with someone in the other camp might help sort out the matter without relations deteriorating any further?

Remain objective

This would seem to be the same point as above, but even senior members of staff can find themselves infuriated by a debtor's behaviour and start to unconsciously make irrational decisions to recover a debt oblivious to the actual chances of recovery and cost to their own business. Financial disputes can become emotive very quickly but an effective recovery should be based on objective assertiveness.

Fixed-price advice

Check your current situation and the chances of success before getting locked into an expensive long-term litigation. If you know there is a dispute but you have reservations about the matter, take fixed-price legal advice before issuing a claim. Too many claims have been issued over the years without the decision-makers taking proper advice and double-checking the realities of proceeding via legal paths and have found themselves met with a counterclaim. The result of not taking proper fixed-price advice is all too often that the creditor ends up locked into potentially expensive litigation when they need not have been.

Part 5

Credit management for export markets

$$B_2 B_2 B \cdot (INT)^* =$$

**The most powerful formula
for (international) debt recovery**

BIERENS
DEBT RECOVERY LAWYERS

* Business to Business to Bierens x international

Cross-border debt recovery – breaking down the barriers

John Holmes, Bierens Incasso Advocates

Although there are differences between the legal systems of the United Kingdom and the rest of the European Union (EU), since the introduction of the European Order for Payment (EOP) procedure in December 2008 (EC Regulation 1896/2006 – 'the Regulation'), recovering cross-border commercial debts in the EU has been simplified. The procedure, although restricted to undisputed cross-border claims, is the latest in a string of initiatives designed to facilitate the swift and efficient recovery of outstanding debts within the EU.

With the exception of Denmark, the procedure applies to all EU member states and is available as an alternative to existing national procedures. As at least one of the parties must be domiciled in another EU member state, it cannot be used within the United Kingdom, for example between an English creditor and a Scottish debtor. In addition, the procedure cannot be used in respect of property rights arising out of a matrimonial relationship, wills and succession, bankruptcy, social security or claims arising from non-contractual obligations (Article 2 of the Regulation). However, there is no limit to the value of the claim and, subject to both EU and national rules, it is also possible to claim interest and costs in addition to the principal debt.

The dilemma

Company A in Birmingham has entered into a contract with company B in Lisbon, Portugal, for the manufacture and sale of car parts. A term of the contract is that Portuguese law and the Portuguese courts shall have jurisdiction. Although company A has supplied the goods and company B has accepted them, company B argues that they can no longer pay for them owing to cash flow problems. What can company A do in order to recover its money quickly and cost effectively?

A number of thoughts spring to mind. First, the debtor is abroad and, perhaps, you have no idea of what your legal rights are in Portugal. The culture, language and courts are different. How much will it cost, and will it take forever to recover the debt? In short, you are now in unfamiliar territory and panic begins to set in. However, that does not have to be the case.

The EOP procedure

The first question in any international dispute is to establish which law applies to the contract and which member state has jurisdiction to adjudicate the claim. In the example above, the answer is straightforward as both parties have agreed to Portuguese law and to Portuguese jurisdiction. In other cases, this question may not be so easy to determine and legal advice should be sought before proceeding further.

The application itself consists of completing a standard form (form A), which can be downloaded from the EU Commission website (http://ec.europa.eu/justice_home/judicialatlascivil/html/epo_information_en.htm), and is set out in the same format and language for each member state. In this example, since the application has to be lodged at the Portuguese court, the Portuguese form must be completed rather than the English equivalent. As the format of the form is identical for each member state, this is not difficult to complete even though the language is different. The application is also based on the no-evidence model, and only requires the claimant to list the evidence upon which he relies, with no requirement to actually enclose that evidence (this is optional in the United Kingdom). The form, once completed, is then sent, with the court fee, by post to the Portuguese court seized with determining the application. The EU website contains information about which court is empowered to determine EOP applications in the EU.

Upon receipt of the application, the competent court normally has 30 days within which to determine if the information supplied complies with the requirements of the Regulation. If it does not comply with the requirements, it will be rejected; otherwise the court will issue the EOP, using standard form E. If the claim is rejected, then you can resubmit the application rectifying the earlier defect. There are no limits as to how many times you can resubmit the application. Once accepted, the EOP (form E) is served on the defendant in accordance with national law and the defendant is notified of its options. The defendant has 30 days within which to pay the debt or object to the order. If the defendant fails to pay or does not respond at all, then the court will issue standard form G entitling the claimant to execute the order.

However, and perhaps this is the largest drawback of the EOP procedure, a defendant can oppose the order without having to give reasons. The debtor simply has to tick a box and then return the EOP to the court. Nevertheless, unless the claimant has notified the court otherwise, an opposed claim is automatically transferred to the member state's normal civil litigation procedures, where the defendant would then be required to give reasons for their objection or face summary judgment. Automatic transfer is introduced to remove the problem of a claimant having to start all over again, and to ensure that sooner or later the defendant has to give reasons for their objection rather than simply walking away from its responsibilities.

In most cases, as in the example above, the Portuguese company is unlikely to oppose the granting of the order, as the reason for non-payment is that they cannot pay as opposed to the existence of a substantive legal dispute. In a case where there is a legal dispute, for example because the goods were faulty, then the EOP procedure would be unavailable in any event. Thus, the idea behind the EOP is to ensure that where non-payment is the only reason behind settlement of the debt, difficulties in understanding national proceedings can be set aside by the use of a standard procedure that follows the same rules in each member state.

Execution of an EOP

In the event that company B fails to respond or fails to pay the debt within 30 days of the granting of the order, and has failed to object to it being granted, then, upon receipt of form G from the court, company A can immediately commence execution proceedings in Portugal.

Assume for one minute that English law and jurisdiction had applied to the contract, and the procedure had been followed in England as outlined above (using the English forms), then once the court has issued form G, the EOP should be immediately recognizable in Portugal and can be executed in Portugal as if it were a Portuguese judgment. Thus, the domicile of the defendant should not be a barrier to the effective administration of justice. It may take slightly longer to complete the procedure, because, for example, of the need to comply with the requirements for the service of legal documents abroad, but the same EOP principles that apply in Portugal apply equally in England, and the cross-border nature of the claim should no longer be a barrier to the effective recovery of cross-border debts.

Once the order has been issued (form E) and execution confirmed by the issue of form G, then execution of the order is carried out in accordance with national rules and procedure. At this stage, advice should be sought as to which form of execution procedure is suited to the circumstances of the individual claim, as national rules will apply.

Alternatives to the EOP in the EU

The EOP procedure has been introduced as an alternative procedure and should not be seen as being the only method available to quickly and efficiently recover debts. The member state within which the defendant is domiciled may have an alternative procedure that is more advantageous.

The EOP procedure, although an entirely new concept for some countries, and most notably in the United Kingdom, has been modelled on a number of order for payment procedures that already existed in other member states.

Portugal, for instance, offers a similar order for payment procedure (procedimento de injunção), and in some cases the route to judgment can be achieved in almost half the time than that of an EOP application.

The Portuguese order for payment application is completed online by a Portuguese lawyer. The entire proceedings can be tracked online and, as such, it increases the efficiency of the legal process. By using this procedure, court fees are also reduced by between 25 per cent and 50 per cent. Once the application has been sent electronically to the national order for payment office, it is usually verified within five days and the claim is subsequently served on the defendant. The defendant then has 15 days within which to pay the debt or object to the claim. As with the EOP procedure, if the defendant fails to pay the debt and does not object to the order, then the claimant's legal representative is notified of this fact, and an executable order is granted. This entitles the claimant to immediately commence execution proceedings, which usually takes the form of a seizure of assets.

Statistically, 91 per cent of order for payment applications are granted and 85 per cent result in the issue of an executable order. In addition, 55 per cent of all claims relate to debts of less than €500, which shows that the system is also suited for both large and small claims (Source: Direcção-Geral de la Política de Justiça, June 2009).

Portugal is by no means an isolated example. Other EU member states operate similar order for payment procedures. In Latvia, for example, the equivalent to the EOP is the warning procedure; in Germany, the mahnverfahren; or in Hungary, the payment order procedure. All follow a similar theme and are similarly based on the no-evidence model.

More information about simplified and accelerated procedures can be found on the EU website at http://ec.europa.eu/civiljustice/index_en.htm.

Advantages and disadvantages to the EOP

Like any new system there are bound to be teething problems, and the EOP is by no means an exception. However, it would be an exaggeration to suggest that the application first has to get past the 'judicial assassin' before the EOP is issued [NLJ 159/7353 p.108]. The application form is set out in such a user-friendly way that, if all the correct information is supplied, there is very little a judge can do to 'kill it off'. That being said, there are one or two EU member states that have had more difficulty than others in adapting to the new regime. Most notably, the Irish

High Court has, to date and without reason, failed to deal with a number of applications; and in Spain, inadequate implementation and the lack of judicial training has resulted in a number of courts incorrectly processing EOP applications under the national proceso monitorio procedure, resulting in unnecessary technical and administrative delays.

Notwithstanding the above, initial experience of the EOP in other EU member states has been positive. First, Italy, notorious for its perceived entangled bureaucracy, has embraced the EOP procedure and opened the way to effective debt recovery. Secondly, both the English and Scottish courts have had little trouble with issuing an EOP.

Furthermore, the main advantage to the EOP procedure, apart from the speed with which an order can be issued, is that it is possible (subject to questions of applicable law and jurisdiction) to obtain an order in the host member state, for example England, which can then be executed in, for example, France. Alternatively, it may also be possible for an English creditor to use the same procedure directly in France to achieve the same result and greatly speed up cross-border litigation. The language may be different but the legal basis for the EOP is the same.

Ultimately, creditors have been handed an alternative and effective tool to assist in the recovery of their debts. It would seem, therefore, that the EU has taken a step in the right direction to break down the barriers of cross-border debt recovery.

International credit management and debt collection – the use of technology in debt collections

Charles Mayhew, Moreton Smith Limited

Practising good credit management has never been more important in these turbulent times. Moreton Smith have been providing international debt collection and associated credit management services for the last 16 years, on a global basis and for a wide variety of clients. From a sole trader exporting to India, to a listed company selling all over the world, the company has built a network of trusted partners with whom it works on a no-recovery no-fee basis, to make sure that our clients get paid first.

It's a case of what you know, and also much of the time who you know, when dealing with international collection cases.

The role of the professional qualified credit manager has never (certainly in the last 15 years) been more important or more focused upon within the business environment.

We have a saying in the debt collection world that 'prevention is better than cure'. These days companies have far more access to business information on which to base important credit decisions. Business information suppliers, such as Graydon, and Dun and Bradstreet, all have online portals to view not only domestic reports, but also many overseas companies at the click of a mouse.

But where else can you get vital current information on which to base your credit decisions.

One answer is the British Embassies in the country of your debtor. Many of the Embassies have business clubs that are broken down into company segmentations and the Embassy staff will have contacts in each business sector. They may be willing to discuss the relationship that they share with your particular customer.

Also, the International Chamber of Commerce, http://www.iccwbo.org, has a wealth of information and services with which to assist exporters, as does the UK Trade and Investment, https://www.uktradeinvest.gov.uk.

However, what can you do once you have extended credit and are not being paid from a customer, especially when they are based overseas. The perfect answer is to collect your money with interest and retain the goodwill of the customer; anything less than that is not a total solution! An international debt collection agency can recover your funds on a contingency basis and not turn a credit problem into a potentially expensive legal problem. Of course, you sometimes need to refer the debt to a lawyer and enlist their assistance; however, it is important to ask for a time frame as to how long it will take before you may see your funds, and how much it will cost to take the action to recover your funds.

First and foremost, once your company has issued an invoice, telephone the customer to see if the invoice has been received and, importantly, whether or not the invoice is correct. It is at this point that you can ask for a promised date or a date by which the invoice will be settled.

In many larger companies technology plays a large part in the collection process and in many cases companies have used technology to streamline processes in order to reduce headcount and increase cash flow significantly, for example by the use of online payment portals, and interactive e-mails that reduce the need for staff to handle inbound and outbound telephone calls.

One such Moreton Smith customer is Bupa Group, and below you can read the case study on how Bupa achieved success with a technological solution in the form of Hosted Credit Management software. The case study is provided thanks to Martin Kirby, Finance Manager at Bupa.

Bupa Wellness, a subsidiary of Bupa Group, chose to use the MSI collection system in 2007. Previously, Bupa had experienced a decline in collections and required a system that enabled full coverage and gave our team of collectors a 'never forget mentality'. The solution was fully implemented in six weeks. It was really important to the Bupa management team that there was no interruption to day-to-day business and that we combined the functionality of our core system with a collection system that would compliment its standard functionality.

Key requirements

When creating the request for proposal (RFP) Bupa listed the following as key requirements:

■ Fully-hosted solution allowing easy access for up to 50 concurrent users.
■ Collection solution that provides collectors and back-office team with a one-stop shop for all detail and information that they need to engage with the customer.
■ Automated diary system that works in real time.
■ Full dispute module delivering details of the customer dispute to the resolvers, providing an integrated platform for the resolvers then to advise the corrective action required. This needed to be fully auditable with automated-escalation paths.
■ A collection system that would integrate electronic documents such as invoices and customer correspondence and attach them to the relevant transaction, giving the collector the facility to read them and forward them to the customer.
■ Fully customizable reporting that, when defined, could be delivered overnight by e-mail. It was important also that the system recorded the activities of the users and clearly gave management a tool that they could share with collectors to maintain a constant performance.
■ Fully workflow-driven system that executes collection tasks to the users, recording their actions and providing timely reminders and escalation.
■ Online payment portal for B2C customers.

Combining technologies

Notwithstanding the above, Bupa Wellness was already a user of MSI's E-Solutions suite of products. Integrating these products into the collection system has combined both into the one application, reducing our time considerably. It provides a cockpit where the collector can easily drive the agreed strategy, providing the customer with high-quality communications. Customers' comments are captured in the online portal attached to the electronic documents; this then sends those comments, via the workflow engine, back to the collector diary. All this is undertaken without either the customer or the collector needing to telephone each other. The action is then fully recorded as well as time stamped.

Bupa Wellness has achieved the following results:

- double-digit DSO recovery;
- reduced debtors and improved working capital;
- improved customer satisfaction;
- improved collector performance and confidence;
- reduced dispute resolution time;
- full audit compliance.

For more information please see www.moretonsmith.com; the Federation of Small Business – http://fsb.org.uk; The Better Payment Practice Group – http://www.payontime.co.uk.

Limiting credit risk in exports

Jonathan Reuvid, Hethe Management Services

There are basic differences between export sales and domestic business, which, by their nature, have a significant impact on their relative risks. They define the context in which the credit policy and credit management of exporters are set.

In international trade the business environment may be very different: lead times can be much longer; transit times in the carriage of goods or documents can be greater; there may be differences in language, time zones, local customs and laws, working-week cycles and holiday periods, all of which may have an effect on methods of settlement and cash management.

Country risks arising out of political, economic and commercial situations may intervene; there may be inevitable delays in the settlement of insurance and other claims. Until such claims are resolved, problems with the payment mechanism selected may occur. Clearly, it is important to ensure that, as far as is possible, any funding gap generated by the company's export trading activity is not greater in value or time than can be sustained. The associated trade finance cycle and an appropriate choice and structure of related payment mechanisms are critical factors in mitigating risks as well as ensuring effective cash management.

Risk assessment

Chapter 3.2 provides useful guidance on the new services now available through Coface for financial rating on a country basis worldwide, for industry sectors within each territory and for individual companies in a number of countries. Examples of the risk assessments offered by Coface through its website www.Coface.com for 10 selected markets, developed and developing, are shown in Appendix I. These assessments are updated regularly throughout the year and, at this level, are provided free online. When entering a market for the first time or trading in a territory where the economy is unstable or business conditions are deteriorating – a widespread phenomenon during the 2008/09 recession – this website is a valuable first port of call.

In some sophisticated and hopefully 'safer' markets, such as those of the EU, settlement by bank transfer is the norm, but traders should be careful with new customers and if in doubt, insist that letters of credit (L/C) are taken out, at least until a pattern of trade is established. Debt collection and recovery laws and procedures vary considerably from country to country (compare the Czech Republic with Germany in Appendix I) and can be very tedious as well as expensive; so, exporters should take these factors into account before accepting a more relaxed settlement method. The objective must be to reduce the risk of default and debt collection in an export market to a minimum.

Entering a less developed export market is an adventure that inevitably carries risk. Although the exporter may be prepared to bear the risks without insurance, banks and export credit agencies providing export finance may require their customers to take out insurance cover and that will inevitably add to the cost of trading which needs to be built into the contract price.

Methods of payment

The alternative payment methods for the settlement of export invoices vary in the degree of security that they provide to the exporter. The remainder of this chapter summarizes each method and some of the procedures that are involved in the more complex cases.

Advance payment

From an exporter's point of view, an advance payment is ideal for the exporter. Payment is secured in full, in advance of manufacturing or purchasing, the exporter's position is entirely secure and cash flow positive. There are no inherent risks, political or commercial.

However, from the customer's perspective the situation is the reverse of the exporter's. Consequently, the importer will invariably resist advance payment or, having satisfied itself that the exporter is wholly reliable, demand price or other concessions before accepting.

Open account

In an open account situation both the goods and the documents are dispatched by the exporter directly to the importer. The importer receives the goods and, in due course, remits payment to the exporter in a manner agreed upon by both parties, commonly by bank transfer within the EU. Notwithstanding an excellent relationship between the two parties, the potential risks of this procedure are high and it represents the least satisfactory alternative for the exporter. There is a real risk of a delay in the receipt of funds or, in the worst case, the funds not being received in full or at all, with consequent ill effects on cash flow.

Documentary collections

Documentary collections are generally applied where the exporter wishes to secure payment from lesser known but nonetheless reputable importers, making use of the banking system to obtain payment or acceptance of a bill of exchange. (Note the inadequacies of bills of exchange as a secure form of payment in some sophisticated jurisdictions, eg the USA).

The procedures governing the handling of documentary collections through the banking system are covered by the International Chamber of Commerce (ICC) Uniform Rules for Collection.[1] Thankfully, nearly all banks in the commercial world process documents that are submitted to them on a collection basis in accordance with the provisions of these ICC rules.

Typically, an exporter, after shipping the goods, delivers the shipping documents and other appropriate documents to its bank with instructions that they be transmitted to the buyer's bank and be released against payment by the importer or against acceptance of drafts drawn on the importer. Occasionally, additional instructions, eg noting or protesting a bill of exchange or arranging for the storage and insurance of goods, may be given to the exporter's bank, but instructions given by the exporter to its bank must always be full, clear and precise. As a result of this structured and controlled commercial environment, documentary collections generally offer a greater degree of protection to the exporter than open account trading.

Bear in mind, however, that banks are not required to examine documents submitted to them for collection and that the onus is on the exporter to ensure that the documents handed to the bank are in accordance with the requirements of the particular contract, as agreed upon between the importer and exporter. Before shipping the goods, the exporter should ensure that the importer is in possession of the requisite import licence. This import licence must be valid for a period adequate for the goods to be cleared in the country of destination, allowing for any potential delays. Where applicable, the exporter should also verify that current exchange control authorization has been granted to the importer to enable the importer to make payment immediately or at maturity of the usance drafts, in the currency of the collection and in accordance with the instructions contained therein. Documentary collections fall into two main categories:

■ documents against acceptance;
■ documents against payment.

Documents against acceptance (D/A)

With this method, the exporter hands the drafts and accompanying documents to its bank with instructions that the documents be released to the importer in exchange for the importer accepting the drafts for payment at maturity. The drafts would be drawn at a usance[2] agreed upon between the exporter and the importer.

This is where it gets complicated. If the documents do not include documents of title (eg full sets of bills of lading), the position of the exporter is not very much better than in an open account situation, and there is no control over the goods. If the documents include documents of title, control of the goods can be retained by the bank until such time as the drafts have been accepted by the importer, after which time control of the goods is lost.

There are still risks with this method, namely that:

- there may be possible delays in the importer accepting the drafts and the subsequent necessity to warehouse and insure the goods, thus incurring further costs;
- the importer does not accept the drafts and refuses to take up the documents;
- import controls or foreign exchange restrictions (political risks) introduced after shipment of the goods affect the physical import of the goods, or the remittance of the proceeds of the collection upon payment of the drafts at maturity, or both;
- the importer defaults on payment of the accepted draft at maturity.

The exporter may make arrangements with the importer whereby the importer's bank guarantees the payment of the accepted draft by adding its 'for aval' endorsement to the accepted draft. This may be resisted by the importer, who will need to make arrangements with its bank. Be careful to insist that their bank has recognized international status.

Documents against payment (D/P)

The general principle and the process of this method of settlement are similar to the D/A situation, with the exception that the relevant documents are only released to the drawee (the importer) against payment. Control of the goods is therefore retained by the exporter, provided that full sets of documents of title are included in the collection, until such time as payment is made by the importer. However, some of the risks mentioned under the D/A situation still remain.

In the event that the importer is unwilling or unable to take up the goods, or that import controls or exchange control restrictions are introduced after shipment of the goods, the goods may have to be warehoused and insured pending a decision as to their disposal. As in the D/A situation, it is important that full and clear instructions are given to the banks with regard to the warehousing and insurance of the goods in the event that they are not taken up.

Generally, situations in which goods relating to documents forwarded under a documentary collection (whether D/P or D/A) are not taken up by the drawee could prove to be costly to the exporter. This is particularly the case if the goods are manufactured or purchased to special order, are commodities subject to potential large fluctuations in prices, or are perishable goods. In such cases it may not be possible to sell the goods elsewhere or at a loss; therefore the exporter may have to arrange for the goods to be auctioned at the place of discharge, if return of the goods to the exporter is considered to be uneconomic. In any of these circumstances the exporter may suffer a substantial loss.

Documentary credits

In principle, the documentary credit is the most secure payment mechanism both for the exporter and for the importer, provided that it is handled correctly by all parties. The exporter is assured of payment as stated in the credit and the importer is assured that the goods described therein have been shipped. The procedures governing the practice of documentary credits are covered by the ICC's Uniform Customs and Practice for Documentary Credits.[3] Almost all banks in the commercial world transact documentary credit business in accordance with these provisions, referred to as UCP 500. Those intending to use documentary credits in their transactions should familiarize themselves with these procedures.

More recent developments relating to UCP 500 were the introduction by the ICC of two new publications:

■ A supplement known as 'eUCP', which was introduced in January 2002 (ICC Publication No 500/2) and which provides for the electronic presentation of documents. The articles of eUCP are intended to work with UCP 500 where full, or part, electronic presentation of documents takes place.
■ The International Standard Banking Practice (ISBP) for the examination of documents under documentary credits (ICC Publication No 645), which was introduced in January 2003 and which explains how the UCP 500 rules are to be applied.

A documentary credit is an undertaking in writing on the part of the issuing bank made at the request and on the instructions of a customer (the applicant) to make payment to a third party (the beneficiary) of a given sum of money at sight or at some determinable future date against presentation, within a specified time, of certain stipulated documents, provided that the terms and conditions of the credit are complied with. Absolute clarity in instructions given, as well as in the description and nature of the documents required, is essential in order to avoid unnecessary problems.

Note also that a documentary credit is autonomous and a separate transaction from any underlying contracts on which it may be based, even if reference to such contracts is included in the credit. Documentary credits may be issued in revocable or irrevocable form. UCP 500 Sub-Article 6c states that, 'in the absence of such indication the credit shall be deemed to be irrevocable'.

Irrevocable credits

Irrevocable credits cannot be amended or cancelled without the express agreement of all parties to the credit, and thus constitute a definite undertaking on the part of the issuing bank, provided that the stipulated documents are presented to the nominated bank or to the issuing bank and that the terms and conditions of the credit are complied with.

When a credit is also confirmed by another bank (the confirming bank) usually at the beneficiary's location – such confirmation being at the request of, or with the authorization of, the issuing bank – it also bears the undertaking.

Unconfirmed irrevocable credit

When deciding whether to accept an unconfirmed credit or whether to insist that the credit be confirmed by a bank acceptable to the beneficiary, at the beneficiary's location, the exporter should therefore consider both the standing of the issuing bank as well as the country risk.

Confirmed irrevocable credit

The issuing bank risk and country risk are eliminated and the exporter is reliant only on the standing of the confirming bank. In such cases, documents would be presented to the confirming bank, or to any other nominated bank, and drafts would be drawn on the confirming bank or other nominated bank (UCP 500 Sub-Article 9b). This will be referred to again when dealing with risk mitigation.

Of course, it is important to accept as a confirming bank only one of those banks that have recognized international status and to negotiate any amendments to the documentation well in advance of shipment.

Revolving credit

Documentary credits stated as being 'revolving' are reinstated automatically, without further notification after each 'revolution', according to the terms and conditions contained therein. They provide relief from repeated document preparation and administration for exporters who are shipping regularly to the same customer.

Revolving credits take two main forms – those that revolve automatically and those that revolve periodically:

■ A credit that revolves automatically is reinstated after each utilization, until either the maximum amount or the number of revolutions stated are reached.
■ A credit revolving in time (or periodically) would be reinstated after each stipulated period of time had elapsed, again with a stated final expiry date that would take these revolutions into account. For example, a revolving credit for up to 100 units revolving every calendar month would be reinstated for this

amount at the beginning of every successive calendar month until the final stipulated expiry date.

Transferable credits

All the above-mentioned forms of credit can be expressed as being 'transferable', and can be transferred only if expressly designated as transferable by the issuing bank.

Standby letters of credit

Developed in the United States, as a result of legal impediments there concerning the issuing of guarantees, standby letters of credit fulfil a function similar to that of a payment guarantee; they have the character of a 'default instrument' in that payment is triggered by default rather than by performance, as in the case of a documentary credit. Whereas the documentary credit is a payment undertaking, the standby letter of credit is effectively a security against default.

Summary

The core of the advice given in this chapter to exporters is straightforward:

■ Research every export market you enter thoroughly in terms of commercial and political risk.
■ Choose your trade partners carefully, having researched their commercial standing as best you can.
■ Select the method of payment that minimizes the risk of expensive and time-consuming debt collection and recovery in the event of customer default and which the customer will accept.
■ Draft terms of contract accordingly.
■ Ensure that your export documentation is accurate and complete.
■ Examine carefully the credit documentation that your customers, their issuing bank and any confirming bank prepare and negotiate amendments well in advance of shipment.
■ Satisfy yourself that the issuing bank and confirming bank are recognized internationally to ensure acceptance of their documents without question.

More than 50 years ago, the former British Prime Minister Harold Macmillan (later Lord Stockton) famously pronounced that 'exporting is fun'. Having read this chapter, you might very well think otherwise.

Note: Acknowledgments to George Curmi, from whose contributions on trade finance and documentation in Handbook of World Trade, *2003, Kogan Page, much of the information in this chapter is drawn.*

Notes

1 ICC Publication No 522, 1995 revision.
2 Defined by the *Concise Oxford Dictionary* as 'the time allowed by commercial usage for the payment of Foreign Bills of Exchange'.
3 ICC 1993 Revision Publication No 500.

Appendix I – Risk assessment in selected export markets

The information provided in this Appendix are extracts from the country data available without charge on the Coface websites – www.Coface.com – for 10 markets as at 12 December 2009. The countries chosen are all prime export markets and include the United States, Germany as the biggest exporter in the EU, and the Czech Republic as an example of the more recent EU entrants having joined the Community in May 2004. The next four countries selected comprise the so-called BRIC developing markets of Brazil, Russia, India and China. The final three markets reviewed are Saudi Arabia, the largest market of the Middle East, Australia and South Africa, the most developed economy of the region.

In each case, the data presented consist of country and business climate credit ratings, a risk assessment commentary, a checklist of economic assets and weaknesses and, in some cases, a summary of the jurisdiction's means of payment and collection methods.

Other information on the Coface website, not reproduced here, are the major macro-economic indicators, often with current and following year forecasts, commentary on key industries for some developed countries, the main economic indicators for each developing country compared to the regional and developing country averages, with graphs showing insolvency trends to date and a payments incidents index for each country compared to the world average. Together, this information provides exporters and those considering foreign direct investment with a comprehensive background assessment of each local economic climate and trade conditions.

The information in this Appendix is reproduced with the kind permission of Coface UK and Ireland. Readers with more than a passing interest in any market should check www.trading-safely.com or www.Coface.com frequently as the online data is updated regularly.

USA

Country rating: A2

Rating watch listed with negative implications since March 2009.

The political and economic situation is good. ASS basically stable and efficient business environment nonetheless leaves some room for improvement. Corporate default probability is low on average.

Business climate rating: A1

The business environment is very good. Corporate financial information is available and reliable. Debt collection is efficient. Institutional quality is very good. Intercompany transactions run smoothly in environments rated A1.

Risk assessment

The US economy stopped deteriorating in the second quarter (down 0.7 per cent Q/Q annualized), driven mainly by public spending and net exports. Consumption, investment and stocks have continued to undermine growth. The signs of improvement this summer suggest that the economy may be levelling off. The question mark remains, however, whether these signs can evolve into a sustainable trend capable of generating strong growth in 2010. Our scenario is prudent, calling for a soft recovery in 2010 (up 1.3 per cent) for the following reasons:

Household consumption has benefited from temporary government measures (tax credits, social transfer payments, incentives for car purchase and first-time home buyers, for example) and low inflation. There are still risks that could prompt households to spend less, continue paying off debt (down three per cent since 2008) and replenish emergency savings (4.2 per cent in July). The risks include the still high level of household debt (128 per cent of disposable income), an entrenched deterioration of the job market, with the unemployment rate currently 9.8 per cent, the contraction of disposable income associated with resurgent inflation, and an ongoing public deficit.

Housing prices, some recent timid growth notwithstanding, are still very low, down 16 per cent year-on-year in June 2009 and exceeded by household mortgage repayments, with payment defaults and repossessions thus expected to continue and the stock of available homes to remain high (8.5 months).

The recovery of manufacturing production, very dependent on the automotive sector and the cash-for-clunkers programme and on consumer goods sectors, could prove to be just a technical recovery, the destocking phase having been of shorter duration than expected and with companies tending, in view of the existing overcapacity, to remain prudent, gearing their stocks and production as closely as possible to current demand.

Deterioration of the commercial construction sector could ultimately affect bank balance sheets.

Exports (10 per cent of GDP) have not benefited from the stronger economic activity in Asia, particularly China, with that region only providing a market for 19 per cent of sales abroad including 6.0 per cent for China.

Thanks to some drastic cost-cutting starting in the fourth quarter of last year, large companies were able to limit the decline in their rate of profit and significantly improve their cash flow-to-capital expenditures ratio (87.4 per cent decline in 2009 for the rate and 111.6 per cent for the ratio according to Natixisis estimates). They are thus in a position to resume investing and create jobs but have not begun so yet.

The large-company situation has tended to obscure the difficulties encountered by similar companies in gaining access to bank credit. According to the Federal Deposit Insurance Corporation, over 400 of the regional banks that are very close to smaller companies are rated high risks. In this context, corporate bankruptcies will likely continue (up 40 per cent in May 2009 compared to May 2008) notwithstanding the emergence from recession expected in the third quarter. The sectors hit hardest include automotives (dealers and part-makers), residential and commercial construction, and consumer staples (clothing, furniture, leisure and so on), Others such as mechanicals and public works, for example, are, however, expected to begin benefiting by year-end from the vast infrastructure remediation programmes initiated by the Obama administration and local communities.

The fiscal deficit and the federal debt will deteriorate in consequence, increasing respectively to 12.7 per cent and 84.4 per cent of GDP.

Assets

A large market that attracts investors and companies.

Besides inflation, the Federal Reserve Bank also bases monetary policy on economic activity.

Corporate reactivity and flexibility rest on the substantial sector and geographic mobility of the workforce and the flexibility of labour legislation.

The quality of higher education and universities and the size of the high-technology sector contribute to maintaining R&D at a high level and foster the capacity to innovate.

Weaknesses

The economy is highly dependent on property and financial asset values.

The decline in the traditional manufacturing industry tends to keep the current account in deficit.

Very large energy needs makes it crucial to allocate investments focused on adapting to environmental constraints.

Demographic pressures have exposed the inadequacy of health and retirement financing systems.

The poor condition of infrastructure tends to undermine corporate competitiveness.

Means of payment and collection methods

Payments

Exporters should pay close attention to sales contract clauses on the respective obligations of the parties and determine payment terms best suited to the context, particularly where credit payment obligations are involved.

In that regard, cheques and bills of exchange are very basic payment devices that do not allow creditors to bring actions for recovery in respect of 'exchange laws' (*droit cambiaire*) as is possible in other signatory countries of the 1930 and 1931 Geneva Conventions on uniform legal treatment of bills of exchange and cheques.

Cheques are widely used but, as they are not required to be covered at their issue, offer relatively limited guarantees. Account holders may stop payment on a cheque by submitting a written request to the bank within 14 days of the cheque's issue. Moreover, in the event of default, payees must still provide proof of claim.

'Certified cheques' offer greater security to suppliers since the bank certifying the cheque thereby confirms the presence of sufficient funds in the account and makes a commitment to pay it.

Although more difficult to obtain and thus less commonplace, 'cashiers cheques' drawn directly on a bank's own account provide complete security as they constitute a direct undertaking to pay from the bank.

Bills of exchange and promissory notes are less commonly used and offer no specific proof of debt.

The open account system is only justified after a continuing business relationship has been established.

Transfers are used frequently, especially via the SWIFT electronic network – operated by the Society for Worldwide Interbank Financial Telecommunications – to which most American banks are connected and which provides speedy and low-cost processing of international payments.

SWIFT transfers are particularly suitable where trust exists between the contracting parties since the seller is dependent on the buyer acting in good faith and effectively initiating the transfer order.

For large amounts, major American companies also use two other highly automated interbank transfer systems – the Clearing House Interbank Payments System (CHIPS), operated by private financial institutions, and the Fedwire Funds Service System, operated by the Federal Reserve.

Debt collection

Since the American legal system is complex and, especially as regards lawyers' fees, costly, it is advisable to negotiate and settle out of court with customers wherever possible or else hire a collection agency.

The parties can also resort to arbitration or Alternative Dispute Resolutions (ADRs), a relatively informal mediation system, which makes it possible to avoid costly and lengthy ordinary court procedures.

The judicial system comprises two basic types of court: the Federal District Courts, with at least one such court in each State, and the Circuit or County Courts under the jurisdiction of each State.

The *Federal Rules of Civil Procedure* promulgated by the Supreme Court and regularly amended govern the various phases of civil procedure at the federal level, while each State has its own rules of civil procedure.

The vast majority of proceedings are heard by State courts, which apply state and federal law to disputes falling within their jurisdictions (ie legal actions concerning persons domiciled or resident in the State).

Federal courts, on the other hand, rule on disputes involving State governments, cases involving interpretations of the constitution or federal treaties, and claims above US$75,000 between citizens of different American States or between an American citizen and a foreign national or foreign State body or, in some cases, between plaintiffs and defendants from foreign countries.

A key feature of the US judicial system is the pre-trial 'discovery' phase whereby each party, before the main hearing, may demand evidence and testimonies relating to the dispute from the adversary before the court hears the case. During the trial itself, judges give plaintiffs and their lawyers considerable leeway to produce pertinent documents at any time and conduct the trial in general (adversarial procedure).

An amendment to the *Civil Procedure Rules*, in force since 1 December 2006, authorizes document submissions in electronic form (e-discovery), such as e-mail, real-time computer communications, accounting databases, Internet sites and so on.

The 'discovery phase' can last several months, even years, and entail high costs due to each adversary's insistence on constantly providing pertinent evidence (argued by each party), and involves various means – such as examinations, requests to provide supporting documents, the testimony of witnesses and reports by detectives – before submitting them for court approval during the final phase of the proceedings.

Another feature of the American procedural system is that litigants may request a civil or criminal case to be heard by a jury (usually made up of 12 ordinary citizens not familiar with legal aspects – 'twelve good men and true' according to the popular definition of 'jury'), whose task is to deliver a verdict based on the facts of the case and the evidence produced during the proceedings.

In civil cases, the jury determines whether the demand is justified and also determines the penalty to impose on the offender. In criminal cases, the jury decides on the defendant's guilt but the judge decides the punishment.

For especially complex, lengthy or expensive litigation, as in the case of insolvency actions, courts have been known to allow creditors to hold the professionals (eg auditors) counselling the defaulting party liable, where such advisors have demonstrably acted improperly.

Germany

Country rating: A2

The political and economic situation is good. A basically stable and efficient business environment nonetheless leaves room for improvement. Corporate default probability is low on average.

Business climate rating: A1

The business environment is good. Corporate financial information is available and reliable. Debt collection is efficient. Institutional quality is very good. Intercompany transactions run smoothly in environments rated A1.

Risk Assessment

Undermined by the marked weakening of exports, the German economy slipped into recession in spring 2008, a trend expected to continue until autumn 2009, with a timid recovery possibly developing thereafter. Persistently sluggish household consumption will provide little backup support to the economy.

Slumping exports and investment

In the context of a severe breakdown of the world economy and trade, exports, which had been the main growth engine (42 per cent of GDP) until early 2008, are now proving to be the main vector of the recession. Half capital goods (including automotive vehicles) and half consumer goods, the export trend reflects both the end of the investment boom in emerging and raw material producing countries and the downturn of household demand from the major European and American trading partners.

Faced with stagnating exports, eroding margins and tightening credit, German industry will likely put its investments on hold. The downturn is nonetheless unlikely to be excessive in the absence of significant overcapacity and with the release of EUR 18 billion in public loans funded and guaranteed by the *Kredit für Wiederaufhau*. Housing investment is expected, meanwhile, to remain sluggish despite the tax exemption granted for work on home improvements up to EUR 1,200 per year and per household, unlike the public sector investment that will make a positive contribution thanks to federal infrastructure spending and investments loans granted to towns.

Household consumption will also make a slightly positive contribution to growth despite the drop in capital goods purchases such as automotives. Households carry relatively little debt and will not be subjected to a property market downturn. Little deterioration is expected in the job picture, with no substantial increase in unemployment likely. And households will moreover benefit from the delayed effects of wage increases won last year and from easing inflation.

Possible deterioration of payment behaviour

In this unfavourable context, corporate payment behaviour, albeit satisfactory in 2008, could deteriorate in 2009, particularly in sectors heavily dependent on exports such as automotive and aeronautical subcontracting, textile clothing, maritime and river transport and, to a lesser extent, metallurgy, chemicals and industrial capital equipment. The deterioration is nonetheless expected to be limited considering not only the general low debt positions and the substantial equity capital built up in recent years but also the fall of raw material and energy prices.

Assets

Balanced public and social accounts afford additional room for manoeuvre, particularly at a time of crisis.

Public and private efforts on research, already substantial, have been growing.

Smaller German companies – the *Mittelstand* – play a central role in the economy as regards employment, innovation and competitiveness.

'Co-determination' of joint stock companies, mandatory with over 500 employees, has fostered consensus on strategic decisions, particularly involving restructuring.

Good geographic and sector specialization in conjunction with high competitiveness has resulted in a large trade surplus that will doubtless begin to grow again once the crisis is over.

Geographically, nearby Central and European countries that belong to the European Union provide German companies with a wealth of sales and production opportunities.

Weaknesses

Heavily dependent on exports, the German economy is closely tied to world economic conditions.

The plight of the persistently lagging economies of eastern Länder (federated states) is compounded by severe disparities between a north still dependent on traditional economic sectors and a south highly focused on growth sectors.

The family-type businesses prevalent in the Mittelstand complicate matters in obtaining bank financing that must comply with Basel II norms.

Despite merger and acquisition activity spurred by the crisis, the banking landscape remains fragmented, which tends to undermine profitability in the sector.

The inadequacy of facilities for small children has contributed to the low birth rate and ageing of the population, which, in turn, have affected consumption.

The high proportion of youth lacking an adequate general education has resulted in less involvement by companies in apprenticeship programmes – which nonetheless concern two-thirds of the target age group – and in a lack of engineers.

Means of payment and collection methods

Payments

Standard payment instruments such as bills of exchange and cheques are not used very widely in Germany. For Germans, a bill of exchange implies a precarious financial position or distrust on the part of the supplier.

Cheques are not considered a payment as such but as a 'payment attempt'. As German law ignores the principle of covered cheques, the issuer can cancel payment at any time and on any ground. Bounced cheques are therefore fairly common.

Bills of exchange and cheques clearly do not seem to be effective payment instruments even though they entitle creditors to access a fast-track procedure for debt collection.

Bank transfer (*Überweisung*), by contrast, remains the prevalent means of payment. Leading German banks are connected to the SWIFT network, which enables them to provide a quick and efficient funds transfer service.

Debt collection

Since January 2002, the current-law limitation period has been reduced to three years and runs from 1 January of the year following the date the claim came into existence. Limitation periods thus always expire at 31 December of each year.

The collection process begins with the debtor being sent a final demand for payment, via ordinary or registered mail, reminding him of his contractual obligations.

The law on 'speedier matured debts', in force since 1 May 2000, states that where the due date is not specified in the conditions of sale, the customer is deemed to be in default if he does not pay up within 30 days of receipt of the invoice or a demand for payment, and is liable to interest penalties thereafter.

From 1 January 2002, the benchmark default interest rate is the Bundesbank's refinancing rate, plus eight percentage points for retailers or commercial companies and five percentage points for consumers (non-commercial).

If payment or an out-of-court settlement is not forthcoming despite this approach, the creditor must initiate court proceedings.

Provided a claim is payable and uncontested, the creditor can seek an injunction to pay (*Mohnbescheid*) through a simplified and inexpensive procedure involving the use of pre-printed forms accompanied by the documents supporting the claim and resulting in a writ of execution fairly quickly. This procedure has been standardized and automated in most Länder. Foreign creditors must file their claim with the Schönneburg Court in Berlin, which, after examining the claim, may deliver an injunction to pay. The debtor is given two weeks to pay or challenge the injunction (*Widerspruch*).

Ordinary legal proceedings tend to be oral, with the judge reaching his decision on the arguments by both parties in court. If the case is contested, the judge hears the litigants or their lawyers and asks them to submit any evidence deemed relevant by him, which he alone is then authorized to assess. Each litigant is also requested to submit a pleading memorandum outlining his or her expectations, within the specified time limit.

Once the claim has been properly examined, a public hearing is held at which the court hands down a well-found judgment.

The reform of civil procedure, enacted on 1 January 2002, is designed to provide all German citizens with more transparent, timely and effective application of the law.

The new measures encourage parties to attempt reconciliation before resorting to legal action and gives the district courts (*Amtsgerichte*) stronger powers. They also require the majority of cases to be settled in the first instance, either through an out-of-court settlement or through a court decision. An appeal will thus only entail verifying whether a case involves a question of principle or necessitates revision of the law in order to ensure 'consistent jurisprudence'.

The Czech Republic

Country rating: A2

Rating watch listed with negative implications since March 2008.

The political and economic situation is good. A basically stable and efficient business environment nonetheless leaves room for improvement. Corporate default probability is low on average.

Business climate rating: A2

The business environment is good. When available, corporate financial information is reliable. Debt collection is reasonably efficient. Institutions generally perform efficiently. Intercompany transactions usually run smoothly in the relatively stable environment rated A2.

Risk assessment

An economic growth hurt by weakening domestic demand and exports

The economy slumped in 2008. Inflation – fuelled by the increase in VAT and utility prices, as well as in staple commodity prices – undermined consumption. Investment decelerated as a result of the slowdown in domestic and foreign demand. A recession is expected in 2009 amid an upsurge of unemployment, tighter credit conditions and the recession gripping the euro zone, which will further undermine exports and reduce the inflows of foreign direct investment.

These negative trends will largely offset the positive effects of the construction of new automotive factories and the increase in financing from the EU. Inflation will doubtless ease as a result of the sluggishness of domestic demand and drop in raw material prices, which will likely be conducive to reducing interest rates as the Central Bank has been doing since August 2008.

The trade balance will remain in surplus thanks to the weakness of exports. The current account deficit, attributable in large part to income payments to foreign investors, will likely remain limited. Despite the fiscal measures taken, the morose economic conditions will likely keep the government from meeting its objectives on the budget deficit, and all the more so if it implements economic support measures. Government debt will, however, likely remain within reasonable limits (30 per cent of GDP).

Tougher times for companies

The Coface payment incidence for Czech companies has remained below the world average, a slight increase in incidence frequency notwithstanding. Companies suffered in 2008, until July, from the sharp koruna appreciation that squeezed their margins. At this juncture, the main source of concern is the extent to which the growth slowdown and the contraction of European demand will cause some sectors to suffer, particularly transport – already among the weakest – residential construction, and some manufacturing industries, particularly automotives. Pharmaceuticals, meanwhile, have shown great solidity.

A political context not very conducive to reforms

The defeat of Prime Minister Mirek Topolanek's party by the social democratic opposition in the October 2008 regional and senatorial elections, ideological differences and the government's minority status have undermined the centre-right coalition in power. That will be unlikely to facilitate implementation of new reforms, with legislative elections on the horizon (2010). The prime minister was nonetheless re-elected in December to lead his party, which represented a setback for the party's Euro-sceptical wing, personified by the candidate that opposed him for the leadership position and who has close ties to the President of the Republic, Vaclav Klaus.

Assets

European Union membership has enhanced the growth outlook.

Productivity gains, improved fiscal performance and an external financial position benefiting from strong inflows of foreign direct investment left the Czech economy in relatively good shape at the onset of the international financial crisis.

The levels of foreign and public sector debt have remained limited.

The relatively low proportion of loans denominated in foreign currencies limits the exposure of Czech companies to exchange rate risk.

Weaknesses

Highly dependent on foreign trade, the economy is consequently very sensitive to the economic trend in the euro zone.

Profit repatriation by foreign investors undermines the current account.

The shortage of manpower and skills tend to limit growth prospects.

The health and pension systems require additional reforms to strengthen public sector financial sustainability.

The coalition government's weakness could hamper the pursuit of reforms.

Means of payment and collection methods

Payments

Bills of exchange and cheques are not widely used, as they must be in accordance with certain criteria to be valid.

For unpaid and protested bills of exchange (*smĕnka* cizŸ), promissory notes (*smĕnka vlastnŸ*) and cheques, creditors may access a fast-track procedure for ordering payment under which, if the judge admits the plaintiff's application, the debtor has only three days to contest the order against him.

Bank transfers are by far the most widely used means of payment. Leading Czech banks – after successive phases of privatization and concentration – are now linked to the SWIFT system, which provides an easier, quicker and cheaper method for handling domestic and international payments.

Inspired by EU regulations, a recent payment systems law, in force since 1 January 2003, sets the rules for transferring funds in the enlarged European area and empowers the Czech National Bank (*Ceská Národny Banka*) to oversee local use of electronic payment instruments.

Debt collection

It is advisable, as far as possible, not to initiate recovery proceedings locally because of the country's cumbersome legal system, the high cost of legal action and lengthy court procedures – it takes almost three years to obtain a writ of execution due to a lack of judges adequately trained in the rules of the market economy and proper equipment.

Service of final demand for payment supported by proof of debt reminds the debtor of his payment obligations, increased by past due interest payable from the day after the payment date stipulated in the commercial contract.

Since 28 April 2005, the applicable rate, unless agreed otherwise by the parties, is the 'repo' rate applied by the Czech National Bank, in force on the first day of the reference half-year; increased by seven percentage points.

Should the debtor lack the funds needed for immediate payment, it is advisable to seek an out-of-court settlement based on a schedule of payment, preferably drawn up by a public notary accompanied by an enforcement clause that allows them, in case of default by the debtor, to go directly to the enforcement stage, after the court admits the binding nature of that document.

Where creditors have significant proof of claim (unpaid bills of exchange or cheques, acknowledgment of debt, etc), they may obtain an injunction to pay (*plastrební rozkaz*) under a fast-track procedure – which may nonetheless take from three months to a year depending on the workload of the courts, but which does not necessitate a hearing as long as the claim is sufficiently well founded.

The advance on court fees, at the claimant's expense, amounts to four per cent of the total claim.

Where a debtor contests an injunction within 15 days of its service, an ordinary procedure will then apply, with the parties subsequently summoned to one or more hearings to be heard and produce evidence. The judge will then decide whether to throw out the plaintiff's application or order the debtor to pay principal and costs.

Ordinary proceedings are partly in writing, with the parties filing submissions accompanied by all supporting case documents (originals or certified copies), and partly oral, with the litigants and their witnesses heard on the main hearing date.

Any settlement reached between the parties during these proceedings and ratified by the court is tantamount to a writ of execution, in case of subsequent non-compliance with the agreement obtained.

The laws governing commercial companies, commercial papers (bills of exchange, cheques, promissory notes and so on), unfair competition and bankruptcy, for example, fall under the jurisdiction of regional courts (*krajský soud*) or the Prague regional court known as the municipal court (*mesky soud*).

To speed up execution of the excessive number of pending judgments, a new body of bailiffs (*soudní executor*), established since May 2001 and invested with broad investigative powers to identify and locate a debtor's assets before proceeding with actual execution of the court order, is gradually eliminating processing delays.

For that bailiff category, a different fee schedule applies, based on the amount concerned by the execution.

Brazil

Country rating: A4

A somewhat shaky political and economic outlook and a relatively volatile business environment can affect corporate payment behaviour. Corporate default probability is still acceptable on average.

Business climate rating: A4

The business environment is acceptable. Corporate financial information is sometimes neither readily available nor sufficiently reliable. Debt collection is not always efficient and the institutional framework has shortcomings. Intercompany transactions may thus run into appreciable difficulties in the acceptable but occasionally unstable environments rated A4.

Risk assessment

Slumping growth attributable to the international crisis

After remaining strong in 2008, even exceeding the five per cent rate targeted by Brazil's Growth Acceleration Programme (PAC), the economy will suffer a very sharp contraction in 2009, dragged down by the effects of the world economic and financial crisis, despite government stimulus measures, before a mild recovery in 2010. An easing of monetary policy has been underway since early 2009, as the economy is slowing down and real interest rates are still high.

Reappearance of external risks

Weaker export performance attributable to the marked deterioration of the international environment, in conjunction with import vigour, is expected to exacerbate the current account deficit. Liquidity crisis risk will increase due to the very sharp growth of already large external financing needs.

Although foreign direct investment should cover nearly half of these needs, for the balance Brazilian companies will experience greater difficulty in obtaining financing abroad in 2009 than in past years. The confidence of financial markets has been shaken, as reflected by the sharp increase in risk premiums (spreads) and the very high volatility of stock market indices. The USD 30 billion swap currency agreement concluded late 2008 with the US Federal Reserve Bank will likely limit exchange rate instability, and foreign exchange reserves are expected to remain at levels providing Brazil with a solid safety net. Moreover, a well-capitalized banking sector – strengthened by a US\$ 50 billion infusion of liquidity and the Itaú/Unibanco merger – apparently has little exposure to the toxic effects of derivative products.

Private foreign debt is expected to grow substantially, but with the public debt reduced portion, Brazil's external vulnerability has eased albeit with the foreign debt service burden remaining significant in proportion to exports. Moreover, while the structure of the domestic public debt continues to improve, the public debt remained too high at 55 per cent of GDP in gross terms in 2008, notably impeding investment and infrastructure modernization.

Lagging pace of reforms in the run-up to the presidential election in late 2010

The adoption of the structural reforms necessary to sustainable development has lagged due to the parliamentary coalition's heterogeneous composition and a lack of commitment on the part of the government in the run-up to the presidential election scheduled in October 2010, with the incumbent President Lula da Silva barred by the Constitution from running for a third term.

Signs of deteriorating payment behaviours

In this context, companies are hampered by credit restrictions (particularly small and medium-sized enterprises) and/or the exchange rate trend in regular business transactions or due to debt contracted in foreign currencies and their payment behaviour will likely suffer in consequence.

Some sectors continue to face chronic difficulties, as is the case for the garment and footwear industries grappling with foreign competition. In other sectors the more difficult economic conditions have taken their toll, as in agribusiness, the mining and steel industries, construction, automotives (car makers, parts manufacturers, dealers) and mass distribution (particularly in home appliances and information technology).

Assets

Brazil is endowed with extensive and varied natural resources and its economy has been diversifying.

Manufactured products represent a growing proportion of production and exports.

Policy continuity on the pursuit of macroeconomic stability seems assured.

The capacity to cope effectively with international finance market volatility has increased.

Brazil's domestic market potential and competitive labour costs enhance its attractiveness to foreign investors.

Weaknesses

To achieve sustainable growth, structured reforms will be necessary – notably in education, social security, the employment market, taxation and the regulatory framework, but they have come up against major political obstacles.

A lack of investment has resulted in deficient energy, rail, road, port and airport infrastructures, with public–private partnerships difficult to set up.

Brazil remains exposed to fluctuations in world prices for certain commodities.

Public debt remains high and exposed to domestic interest rate trends, with its maturity still too short.

Russia

Country rating: C

A very uncertain political and economic outlook and a business environment with many troublesome weaknesses can have a significant impact on corporate payment behaviour. Corporate default probability is high.

Business climate rating: B

The business environment is mediocre. The availability and reliability of corporate financial information vary widely. Debt collection can sometimes be difficult. The institutional framework has a few troublesome weaknesses. Intercompany transactions run appreciable risks in the unstable, largely inefficient environments rated B.

Risk assessment

Impact of the credit crunch

The financial crisis hit the Russian economy hard in autumn 2008, with the rouble and stock market indices falling and the interbank market in gridlock. The government intervened via state-run banks to bolster companies faced with heavy debt service denominated in foreign currency.

Repayment of private debt will remain a risk that bears watching in 2009, with companies and banks having accumulated considerable debt owed to foreign creditors (syndicated bank loans or Eurobonds). In the context of aversion to risk that will still prevail in 2009/2010, refinancing the debt will be no easy matter. With foreign exchange reserves still large and public sector debt limited, government officials have the means to intervene to stem a wave of defaults.

In the banking sector, however, there are still too many under-capitalized actors alongside state-run banks, with the lack of reforms making it very vulnerable to a crisis of confidence. And it is not certain that the crisis will provide the impetus for the necessary restructuring. As such, bank credit, which has been very dynamic in recent years, will likely suffer a profound slowdown.

Economic weakness

In this context, the economy has been in a marked slowdown phase since late 2008, with GDP growth contracting highly in 2009. Household consumption, the main economic engine since 2000, will decelerate sharply amid increasingly scarce credit and falling prices of oil, which had contributed to the explosive growth of household incomes. And the first wage payment failures had already begun to occur towards the end of 2008. The falling prices will moreover not only hobble oil production; they will no longer be able to mask the stagnation of production that was already apparent in 2008, a trend attributable to the lack of investment in the energy sector.

The current economic slowdown will particularly weaken retailing, automotives and a metals sector where prices have also been falling. By end 2008, companies in these sectors announced staff reductions and a drop in production.

Deteriorating corporate payment behaviour

Coface monitoring records on Russian companies reflect a deterioration of their payment behaviour even before the international financial crisis began to have a tangible impact on the economy.

That trend is attributable to persistent corporate governance difficulties, with the instability of ownership structures, the weakness of the courts and, particularly, of creditor protection, and the relative opacity of corporate accounts continuing to mark the business environment.

In this difficult context, the economic slowdown and the problems facing some sectors are expected to spur a new surge of payment failure in 2009/2010.

Assets

Russia is endowed with a wide range of natural resources (oil, gas, metals, diamonds),

With low public sector debt and the world's third largest foreign exchange reserves, the government has room for manoeuvre.

The 2014 Olympic Winter Games in Sochi offer an opportunity to develop infrastructures and enhance the country's attractiveness to tourists.

Russia has reasserted its regional and energy power status while benefiting from notable political stability.

Weaknesses

The banking sector has undergone few reforms.

The industrial sector lacks competitiveness, particularly on quality.

The growing number of companies coming under state control could undermine their development and result in ineffective management.

Reforms adapted in general are either not implemented or in many cases diverted from their original purpose to serve the interests of business circles.

India

Country rating: A3

Changes in a generally good but somewhat volatile political and economic environment can affect corporate payment behaviour. A basically secure business environment can nonetheless give rise to occasional difficulties for companies. Corporate default probability is quite acceptable on average.

Business climate rating: A4

The business environment is acceptable. Corporate financial information is sometimes neither readily available nor sufficiently reliable. Debt collection is not always efficient and the institutional framework has shortcomings. Intercompany transactions may thus run into appreciable difficulties in the acceptable but occasionally unstable environments rated A4.

Risk assessment

India shows resilience during current economic downturn

Growth slowed in 2008, reaching 6.5 per cent (vs nine per cent in 2007). Consumption suffered from a worsening job picture and a negative wealth effect associated with the fall of stock market and property prices. Tightening credit conditions have, moreover, affected investment. Besides, foreign demand from industrialized countries and emerging Asia has slumped. On the supply side, performance sagged somewhat in industry, notably the automotive sector, and services. The fall of property prices by as much as 30 per cent in some cities has weakened the construction sector. In this context, corporate payment behaviour, which had improved in recent years according to Coface records, has slightly deteriorated amid a still noteworthy lack of transparency in financial reporting by mid-size companies and the absence of consolidated balance sheets for groups.

In 2009, GDP growth is expected to remain at a satisfactory level (5.5 per cent) thanks to the low degree of openness of the economy and to expansionary fiscal and monetary policies. Indeed, improvement signs are already perceptible (Q1 2009 growth of 5.8 per cent vs 5.1 per cent during Q4 2008).

However, companies are calling for external financing and a prolonged scarcity of the credit on international financial markets could affect them. In the event of a new crisis, payment defaults could rise.

Public sector finances remain India's main weakness

Public sector finance deficit increased in 2008 amid economic slowdown. Although in sharp decline, public sector debt is still high and the heavy debt service burden continues to undermine public sector capital investment.

The current account deficit widened in 2008 amid rising oil prices and declining transfers from expatriate workers. The current account deficit will, however, likely narrow in 2009 thanks to the decline in raw material prices. And net foreign direct investments will continue to cover financing needs that have been stable despite the international financial turbulence. Besides, portfolio investments (very volatile in 2008) are expected to stabilize in 2009. Finally, with its foreign exchange reserves remaining at good levels, India will be well equipped to withstand any sudden capital flight.

More structural reforms expected after the 2009 general elections

India held general elections between 26 April 2009 and 13 May 2009. The incumbent United Progressive Alliance (UPA) coalition, which the Congress party leads, has won an overwhelming victory. India's new government is now likely to be more cohesive and will have as greater leeway to implement structural reforms.

Assets

India is endowed with diversified growth engines ranging from investment and exports to strong consumption by an emerging middle class.

Economic growth rests on solid fundamentals, with already high savings and investment rates (over 35 per cent) increasing steadily.

India's private companies are its main asset as much in industry (pharmaceuticals, car industry, textiles) as in services (information technology, outsourcing) and their satisfactory profitability is indicative of a well-positioned productive apparatus.

The country benefits from moderate foreign debt and ample foreign exchange reserves.

Weaknesses

The public sector financial position remains India's main weakness, with the debt service draining a high proportion of fiscal revenues to the detriment of development spending.

A lack of infrastructure (electricity and transport) remains an obstacle to a faster pace of growth,

The deficiencies of the education system and the scarcity of trained workers have tended to drive up the wages of skilled labour, which could ultimately erode India's competitive advantage.

The rapid increase in the debt carried by private Indian companies will bear watching.

The Kashmir question has not yet given rise to conclusive negotiations and remains a major element of uncertainty in historically conflict-prone relations with Pakistan. The November 2008 bombing in Mumbai could, furthermore, heighten the tensions between Pakistan and India.

China

Country rating: A3

Changes in a good but somewhat volatile political and economic environment can affect corporate payment behaviour. A basically secure business environment can nonetheless give rise to occasional difficulties for companies. Corporate default probability is quite acceptable on average.

Business climate rating: B

The business environment is mediocre. The availability and reliability of corporate financial information vary widely. Debt collection can sometimes be difficult. The institutional framework has a few troublesome weaknesses. Intercompany transactions run appreciable risks in the unstable, largely inefficient environments rated B.

Risk assessment

Economic slowdown in 2008

After peaking in 2007 with 13 per cent annual growth, the Chinese economy cooled in 2008 amid a slowdown of exports and domestic demand. Export growth slowed somewhat as a result of sagging demand from industrialized countries, which absorb 46 per cent of total sales abroad. Consumption declined meanwhile essentially as a result of growing inflation in S1 2008 and rising unemployment. And the reduced dynamism of investment is attributable to the narrowing of corporate margins, particularly in sectors with overcapacity (steel, car industry, real estate, etc).

Gradual recovery in 2009 thanks to effective fiscal and monetary policies

To deal with the slowdown, the government has adopted a more expansionary monetary policy (removal of limits on credit growth, lowering of interest rates and reserve requirements). Since late 2008 officials have similarly shifted gears on exchange rate policy to foster stabilization of the Yuan and bolster export sectors in difficulty. And with the leeway afforded by low public sector debt (18 per cent of

GDP) and a high savings rate, the government has decided to implement a USD 586 billion fiscal stimulus devoted to major infrastructure projects – with investments in transportation and electricity, reconstruction of areas devastated by the earthquake, among others – and social measures (education, subsidies to rural populations, housing aid, etc).

After reaching its lowest level in Q1 2009 (6.1 per cent y/y vs 6.8 per cent y/y in Q4 2008), GDP growth rebounded in Q2 2009, reaching 7.9 per cent y/y. This recovery has been driven predominantly by domestic demand. Indeed, public capital formation has substituted for private investment and private consumption has held up reasonably well. However, net exports have not contributed to growth.

The economic recovery is expected to continue in H2 2009 and 2010. GDP growth is thus expected to reach 8.5 per cent in 2009 and 10 per cent in 2010.

Default risk that will bear watching in 2009

Despite the fiscal stimulus, the risk of payment failures in particular sectors will nonetheless remain substantial. Indeed, the huge fiscal stimulus has led to major structural changes. China focuses increasingly on high-level range industries. In some sectors, especially the ones in low value-added industries (textiles, shoes, toys) and the industries suffering from over-capacity (automotive, construction, steel), the number of actors will decrease. These sectors will concentrate most of payment default risks. According to Coface monitoring records, payment behaviour has been deteriorating, a trend likely to worsen in 2009.

Besides, the social and political upheavals attributable to the widening gap between urban and rural areas and the upsurge of unemployment in the context of a slowing economy will bear watching.

Assets

China's external financial position has benefited from its competitive and diversified industry.

Foreign investments have facilitated a gradual move upmarket.

The development of infrastructure, galvanized by the preparations for the 2008 Olympic Games in Beijing and the huge fiscal stimulus implemented in November 2008, provides support for long-term growth.

A huge corporate savings rate has enabled companies to fund most investments.

China's growing influence in the international arena is a readily observable fact.

Weaknesses

The rise of inequality has stoked growing social tensions.

Overcapacity has jeopardized several industrial and commercial sectors.

Despite progress on prudential regulations and the entry of foreign investors, Chinese banks remain weak in view of the rapid credit expansion and uncertainties over the non-performing loans.

Environmental problems hinder the development of sustainable growth. The Taiwan issue remains a significant factor of risk.

Saudi Arabia

Country rating: A4

A somewhat shaky political and economic outlook and a relatively volatile business environment can affect corporate payment behaviour. Corporate default probability is still acceptable on average.

Business climate rating: B

The business environment is mediocre. The availability and reliability of corporate financial information vary widely. Debt collection can sometimes be difficult. The institutional framework has a few troublesome weaknesses. Intercompany transactions run appreciable risks in the unstable, largely inefficient environments rated B.

Risk assessment

A solid financial position

Driven by booming oil prices, the revenues raked in these past years have facilitated implementation of vast infrastructure projects, an increase in oil production capacity, a reduction of government debt and a build-up of financial assets. The kingdom is now in a very strong economic and financial position, expected to allow it to cope with the consequences of the world economic crisis that began to appear in 2008 with the fall of stock market indices and capitalizations, and the drop in the oil price from July on, in conjunction with a shortage of liquidity and a weakening of foreign demand. In this context, strong growth in the first half, buoyed by a sharp increase in oil production, subsequently showed signs of slowing down, particularly in the petrochemical and oil sectors.

The economic downturn and the credit crunch affected household consumption and prompted private investors to cancel or postpone some projects. With inflation easing late in the year, officials took measures to increase liquidity and to stimulate the economy. And bank deposits are moreover guaranteed by the government.

Oil revenues under pressure in 2009

The leading OPEC oil-producing country, Saudi Arabia will likely continue in 2009 to make the most of the adjustment effort for the downward world-demand trend. Oil production could thus decline compared to 2008. The non-oil sector will thus be the sole growth engine and continue to benefit from large public sector investment projects likely to be funded from the financial reserves accumulated these past years. Some projects, however, could be delayed. Public spending, subsidies and social aid are expected to buoy household consumption and living standards, thus protecting the social climate. In 2009 the contraction in oil production, however, will lead to a recession and the recovery in 2010 will probably be moderate.

The business climate improved with Saudi Arabia's admission to the WTO in late 2005. But it continues to suffer from persistent weaknesses in governance terms. The performance of companies could suffer from the economic slowdown, with deterioration of their payment behaviour not unlikely in view of their traditional vulnerability to a downturn of barrel prices.

With barrel prices substantially below their average levels in 2008, a decline in hydrocarbon production will likely result in a sharp drop in export earnings and fiscal revenues, which will still derive mainly from oil. The public sector and current account balances will consequently be far below their levels of past years. The country will likely be able to cope effectively with the economic downturn, since it starts from a solid financial position.

Assets

The number one OPEC oil producer, Saudi Arabia occupies a strategic position in the markets. That strategic position in conjunction with its regional economic and political throw-weight has made the kingdom a privileged interlocutor for the United States.

The country has been opening up to foreign investment.

Its financial position is sufficiently solid to enable it to cope with external shocks.

Weaknesses

The growth of oil sector production (with its 'swing-producer' role in adjusting to world demand and OPEC policy) has been erratic.

Conservative traditions have impeded political and economic liberalization.

Strong demographic growth and an unsuitable education system have resulted in high unemployment that could jeopardize the social climate.

Regional geographical instability has weighed on the investment environment.

Australia

Country rating: A2

The political and economic situation is good. A basically stable and efficient business environment nonetheless leaves room for improvement. Corporate default probability is low on average.

Business climate rating: A1

The business environment is very good. Corporate financial information is available and reliable. Debt collection is efficient. Institutional quality is very good. Intercompany transactions run smoothly in environments rated A1.

Risk assessment

The economy improved slightly in the 2009 first quarter (up 0.14 per cent y/y) thanks to a range of government support measures intended for households (tax rebates, aid to first-time property owners) and companies. Other factors have contributed to Australia's economic strength, including: steady iron ore and coal exports buoyed by the high prices prevailing in recent years and reductions in the Central Bank's key rates, which have spurred consumption by households by reducing their debt service burden.

But the recent downward renegotiation (over 30 per cent) of prices associated with raw material shipments and the tendency cultivated by China these past weeks to operate in commodity futures markets to meet its supply needs is expected to undermine mining company exports and investment. Saddled with heavy debt averaging 156 per cent of disposable income, households will continue to exercise extreme caution on spending (deterioration of the labour market and priority given to replenishing emergency savings) and to repay debt. Economic growth is expected to contract nearly one per cent this year.

Means of payment and collection methods

As a former colony of the British Crown, Australia's legal system and legal precepts are broadly inspired by British 'common law' and the British court system. On 1 January 1901, the six British colonies formed the dominion of Australia as an independent union within the Commonwealth.

Payments

Bills of exchange and promissory notes are not widely used in Australia and are considered, above all, to authenticate the existence of a claim. Cheques, defined as 'bills of exchange drawn on a bank and payable on presentation', are commonly used for domestic and even international transactions.

SWIFT bank transfers are the most commonly used payment method for international transactions. The majority of Australian banks are connected to the SWIFT electronic network, offering a rapid, reliable and cost-effective means of payment.

The Australian dollar, along with the main foreign currencies, is now also part of the Continuous Linked Settlement Scheme (CLS), a highly automated interbank transfer system for processing international trade settlements.

Moreover, the handling of payments via the client bank's internet site is becoming increasingly commonplace.

Debt collection

The collection process starts with the service of an order to pay via a registered 'seven-day letter', reminding the client of his obligation to pay the amount due plus any contractually agreed interest penalties or, lacking such a penalty clause, interest at the legal rate applicable in each state.

In the absence of payment by the debtor company and if the creditor's claim is due for payment, uncontested, and over AUS$ 2,000 (or after a ruling has been made), the creditor company may issue a summons demanding payment within 21 days. Unless the debtor settles the claim within the required time frame, the creditor may lodge a petition for the winding-up of the debtor's company, considered insolvent (statutory demand under section 459E of the Corporations Act 2001).

Under ordinary proceedings, once a statement of claim (summons) has been filed and where debtors have no grounds on which to dispute claims, creditors may solicit a fast-track procedure enabling them to obtain an enforcement order by issuing the debtor with an 'application for summary judgment'.

This petition must be accompanied by an affidavit (a sworn statement by the plaintiff attesting to the claim's validity) along with supporting documents authenticating the unpaid claim.

For more complex or disputed claims, creditors must instigate standard civil proceedings, an arduous, often lengthy process lasting up to two years given the fact that the court systems vary from one state to another.

During the preliminary phase, the proceedings are written insofar as the court examines the case documents attesting to the parties' respective claims. During the subsequent 'discovery phase', the parties' lawyers may request their adversaries to submit any proof or witness testimony that is relevant to the matter and duly examine the case documents thus submitted.

Before handing down its judgment, the court examines the case and holds an adversarial hearing of the witnesses, who may be cross-examined by the parties' lawyers.

Local Courts or Magistrates Courts (depending on the State) hear minor disputes involving amounts ranging from a minimum AUS$ 40,000 in the State of South Australia up to a maximum AUS$ 100,000 in the States of Victoria or Northern Territory.

Beyond these various thresholds, disputes involving financial claims up to AU$ 675,000 in New South Wales, AU$ 500,000 in Western Australia or AU$ 250,000 in Queensland, for example, are heard either by the County Court or District Court, depending on the State. Claims equal to those threshold amounts or greater are heard by the Supreme Court of each State. Since January 2007, the State of Victoria has granted the County Court the jurisdiction to hear disputes irrespective of size of claims involved.

As a general rule, appeals lodged against Supreme Court decisions, where a prior ruling in appeal instance has been handed down by a panel of judges, are heard by the High Court of Australia, in Canberra, which may decide, only with 'leave' of the court itself, to examine cases of clear legal merit. The right of final recourse before the Privy Council, in London, was abolished on 3 March 1986 (Australia Act 1986).

Lastly, although the Australian legal system does not have commercial courts per se, in certain States, such as New South Wales, commercial sections of the District or Supreme Courts offer fast-track proceedings for commercial disputes.

Since 1 February 1977, Federal courts have been created alongside the State courts and established in each State capital. The federal courts have wide powers to hear civil and commercial cases (like company law, winding up proceedings), as well as fiscal or maritime matters, intellectual property, consumer law, and so on. In certain cases, the jurisdictional boundaries between State and Federal Courts may be indistinct and this may lead to conflicts, depending on the merits of each case.

Arbitration and Alternative Dispute Resolution (ADR) procedures may also be used to resolve disputes more rapidly and obtain out of court settlements, often at a lower cost than through the ordinary adversarial procedure.

South Africa

Country rating: A3

Rating watchlisted with negative implications since June 2008.

Changes in a generally good but somewhat volatile political and economic environment can affect corporate payment behaviour. A basically secure business environment can nonetheless give rise to occasional difficulties for companies. Corporate default probability is quite acceptable on average.

Business climate rating: A3

The business environment is relatively good. Although not always available, corporate financial information is usually reliable. Debt collection and the institutional framework may have some shortcomings. Intercompany transactions may run into occasional difficulties in the otherwise secure environments rated A3.

Risk assessment

Slumping household consumption and exports

Economic growth fell from 5.0 per cent on average these past four years to 3.5 per cent in 2008. Production and investment in the mining sector suffered from power failures in the first quarter, while households – with debt burdens representing over 80 per cent of disposable income – tended to hold back on spending. The economy will likely slow further in 2009 amid a sharp fall in ore prices and sluggish private consumption. The worsening economic conditions are borne out by the deterioration of the Coface payment incident index, with South Africa now rated no better than the world average.

Although inflation, mainly imported from abroad, peaked at 13.6 per cent in August 2008 stoked by surging prices for food and oil products, it has been easing since then, a trend likely to continue in 2009. The Central Bank, doubtless envisaging gradual reduction of its key rate – previously raised 450 basis points between June 2006 and June 2008 – made five rate cuts since December 2008 (the repo rate is currently at 7.5 per cent). The contraction of the current account balance and FED zero interest rate policy should enable the Central Bank to support the internal demands as well as to establish the rand, thanks to the rate discrepancy favourable to trade operations.

Stiffening conditions for financing the current deficit

Thanks to the prudent fiscal policy maintained these past years, the government now has room for manoeuvre in pursuing counter-cyclical policy. The Minister of Finance thus presented a budget for 2009/10 – the first in three years showing a deficit – with spending focused on public investment in infrastructure, transport and energy. The capital goods imports necessary for these investments will contribute, however, to widening the current account deficit, offsetting to some extent the fall of oil prices and the drop in imports of consumer goods, with South Africa's external position weakening in consequence.

The volatility of portfolio investments – which play a preponderant role in financing from abroad – thus increases with the rising risk aversion to emerging risk. Foreign direct investment could similarly begin to wane, with international credit drying up. Multilateral development banks are in this context expected to become a major source of financing in 2009, while external needs could reach US$ 25 billion. With the stiffening conditions for financing the current account tending to exacerbate the rand's volatility, exchange rate risk will in any case remain high in 2009. However, the banking system – relatively unscathed by the subprime crisis – will have little exposure to exchange rate risk in view of the limited extent of positions opened to foreign currency.

Political uncertainties and social risk

With Jacob Zuma – backed by the communist party and unions – winning the presidential election in 2009, the country's future political and economic policies should remain unchanged. However, the leader's ability to reconcile policies apt to reassure the markets with redistribution policies, such as agrarian reform and affirmative action, intended to benefit the historically underprivileged, has met with some scepticism. The social solution, already tense, as evidenced by the xenophobic violence that broke out in June 2008 in Johannesburg and the Cape townships, could deteriorate further with the expected rising of unemployment.

Assets

With the country generating 33 per cent of African GDP, its economic and political influence is an inescapable fact on the continent.

South Africa boasts extensive mining resources, diversified industry and a high-performing tertiary sector (banks, telecommunications, transport).

Public sector finances have been under control, with financing needs moderate and foreign debt limited.

With the country's good creditworthiness, the government has enjoyed substantial capacity to contract new loans.

Tight economic management and the quality of the business environment represent a major asset.

Weaknesses

Under-investment in energy infrastructure has given rise to a chronic energy crisis likely to last for the next five years.

A lack of skilled labour hinders implementation of vast investment projects not only in energy but also in transport.

Although South Africa is one of the main beneficiaries of foreign direct investment in sub-Saharan Africa, the investments nonetheless do not suffice to cover its growing financing needs.

A yawning wage gap reflects the social and economic dualism inherited from apartheid with *Black Economic Empowerment* policies thus far not contributing much to reducing the inequality that stirs social and political tensions.

Appendix II – Contributors' contact list

Amril Limited
2 Chester Avenue
Worthing
West Sussex BN11 2EB
Tel. +44 (0) 1903 215748
Contact: Graham Sands
E-mail: graham.sands@amril.co.uk
Website: www.amril.co.uk

Aon Trade Credit
8 Devonshire Square
London EC2M 4PL
Tel: +44 (0) 20 7882 0146
Contact: Amy Slayford
E-mail: amy.slayford@aon.co.uk
Website: www.aon.co.uk/tradecredit

Bierens Incasso Advocates
PO Box 92
5460 AB Veghel
Zuikade 6
5422 CD Veghel
The Netherlands
Tel: +31 (0) 413 380 980
Fax: +31 (0) 413 351 365
Contact: John Holmes
Direct line: +31 (0) 20 312 11 00
E-mail: j.holmes@bierensgroup.com
Website: www.bierens-incasso-advocaten.com

Coface UK & Ireland
Egale 1
80 St Albans Road
Watford WD17 1RP
Tel: +44 (0) 870 458 2246 / 1923 478111
Fax: +44 (0) 1023 478101
Contact: Xavier Denecker
E-mail: enquiries@cofaceuk.com
Website: www.cofaceuk.com

Graydon UK Ltd
Hygeia Building
66 College Road
Harrow
London HA1 1BE
Tel: +44 (0) 20 8515 1400
Contact: Martin Williams
E-mail: martin.williams@graydon.co.uk
Website: www.graydon.co.uk

Hethe Management Services
Little Manor
Wroxton, Banbury
Oxfordshire OX15 6QE
Tel: +44 (0) 1295 738070
Contact: Jonathan Reuvid
E-mail: jreuvidembooks@aol.com

High Court Enforcement Officers Association
50 Broadway
London SW1H 0RG
Tel: +44 (0) 20 7152 4017
Fax: +44 (0) 20 7152 4001
Contact: Vernon Phillips
E-mail: v.phillips@hceoa.org.uk
Website: www.hceoa.org.uk

The Institute of Credit Management
The Water Mill
Station Road
South Luffenham
Oakham
Leicestershire LE15 8NB
Tel: +44 (0) 1780 722900
Contact: Philip King
E-mail: dg@icm.org.uk
Website: www.icm.org.uk

Jobs In Credit
Foxhall Business Centre
Foxhall Road
Nottingham NG7 6LH
Tel: +44 (0) 115 845 6485
Contact: Brett Marlow
Mobile: +44 (0) 7901 854012
E-mail: brett.marlow@jobsincredit.com
Website: www.jobsincredit.com

Lovetts plc
Bramley House
The Guildway
Old Portsmouth Road
Guildford GU3 1LR
Tel: +44 (0) 1483 457500
Fax: +44 (0) 1483 457700
Contact: Trevor Philips
E-mail: trevorp@lovetts.co.uk
Website: www.lovetts.co.uk

Lowell Group
Enterprise House
1 Apex View
Leeds LS11 9BH
Tel: +44 (0) 845 300 9410
Fax: +44 (0) 845 300 9411
Contact: Joyce Newman
E-mail: joyce.newman@lowellgroup.co.uk
Website: www.lowellgroup.co.uk

Mint Credit Management UK Ltd
Mint House
19 Easton Street
High Wycombe
Buckinghamshire HP11 1NT
Tel: +44 (0) 870 446 0702
Fax: +44 (0) 870 446 0703
Contact: Zoe Lacey
E-mail: zoe@mintcm.com
Website: www.mintcm.com

Moreton Smith Ltd
80 Clerkenwell Road
London EC1M 5RJ
Tel: +44 (0) 20 7490 9010
Fax: +44 (0) 20 7490 9083
Contact: Charles Mayhew
E-mail: charlesmayhew@moretonsmith.com
Website: www.moretonsmith.com

OnGuard
PO Box 125
1394 ZJ Nederhorst den Berg
Slotlaan 3
The Netherlands
Tel: +31 (0) 294 25 66 66
Fax: +31 (0) 294 25 77 33
Contact: Maarten de Wild
E-mail: maarten.de.wild@onguard.com
Website: www.onguard.com

Paladin Commercial Credit Management
35 Chalk Hill
Oxhey
Watford WD19 4B7
Tel: +44 (0) 1923 800397
Fax: +44 (0) 1923 237911
Contact: George Miles
E-mail: George@paladincommercial.co.uk
Website: www.paladincommercial.co.uk

Pricewaterhouse Coopers
Donington Court
Pegasus Business Park
Castle Donington
East Midlands DE74 2UZ
Tel: +44 (0) 150 960 4319
Fax: +44 (0) 150 960 4010
Contact: Niall Cooter
Mobile: +44 (0) 771 406 9861
E-mail: niall.cooter@uk.pwc.com
Website: www.pwc.com/uk/rmg

RBS Invoice Finance
Smith House
Elmwood Avenue
Feltham
Middlesex TW13 7QP
Tel: +44 (0)800 711 911
Fax: +44 (0) 20 8886 7796
E-mail: invoicefinance@rbs.co.uk
Website: www.rbsif.co.uk

Resolvent Ltd
5 St John's Lane
London EC1M 4BH
Tel: +44 (0) 800 011 2686
Contact: Stewart Lund
E-mail: stewart.lund@resolvent.co.uk
Website: www.resolvent.co.uk

TAK-Outsourcing Ltd
PO Box 292
Hampton
Middlesex TW12 9AL
Tel: +44 (0) 20 7100 5978
Contact: Simon Hampton
E-mail: simon.hampton@tak-outsourcing.com
Website: www.tak-outsourcing.com

TALKINGtech UK Ltd
Level 7
3 Harbour Exchange
London E14 9G3
Tel: +44 (0) 20 7987 0101
Fax: +44 (0) 20 7987 0303
Contact: Shaun Maloney
Mobile: +44 (0) 77 6620 0273
E-mail: shaunm@eu.talkingtech.com

Transcom Worldwide (UK)
Transcom House
Alban Park
Hatfield Road
St Albans AL4 0LA
Contact: Mike Purvis
E-mail: mike.purvis@transcom.com
Website: www.transcom.com

UK Payments Administration
Mercury House, Tinton Court
14 Finsbury Square
London EC2A 1LQ
Tel: +44 (0) 20 7711 6228
Contact: Peter Finlayson
E-mail: Petter.Finlayson@ukpayments.org.uk
Website: www.ukpayments.org.uk

Index

Index of advertisers